CRYPTO CLARITY

Mastering Charts and Technical Analysis

AF808794

By

Boyd Alan Sparrow

Crypto Clarity: Mastering Charts and Technical Analysis

CONTENTS

INTRODUCTION 8

CHAPTER 1: UNDERSTANDING THE BASICS OF CRYPTO TRADING 11

Exploring the Crypto Market Landscape 11
Key Players in the Crypto Market 15

CHAPTER 2: UNDAMENTAL ANALYSIS FOR CRYPTO 18

Importance of Crypto Fundamental Analysis 18
Evaluating Crypto Projects and Teams 21

CHAPTER 3: INTRODUCTION TO TECHNICAL ANALYSIS 24

What is Technical Analysis? 24
Differences Between Crypto and Traditional Market Analysis 27

CHAPTER 4: READING CRYPTO PRICE CHARTS 31

Types of Crypto Charts 31
How to Navigate Chart Features 34

CHAPTER 5: UNDERSTANDING CANDLESTICK PATTERNS 38

Basics of Candlestick Patterns 38
Recognising Key Bullish and Bearish Patterns 41

CHAPTER 6: TREND ANALYSIS IN CRYPTO TRADING 44

Identifying Trends in the Crypto Market 44
Utilising Trendlines Effectively 47

CHAPTER 7: SUPPORT AND RESISTANCE LEVELS 51

Defining Support and Resistance 51
How to Identify Support and Resistance on Charts 54

CHAPTER 8: MOVING AVERAGES AND THEIR USES 57

Types of Moving Averages in Crypto 57
Implementing Moving Averages in Your Strategy 60

CHAPTER 9: CRYPTO INDICATORS YOU NEED TO KNOW 64

Introduction to Crypto Trading Indicators 65
Choosing the Right Indicators for Your Analysis 67

CHAPTER 10: THE RSI AND ITS APPLICATION 70

Using RSI for Crypto Trading Decisions 70

CHAPTER 11: MACD: A POWERFUL INDICATOR 74

Understanding the Moving Average Convergence Divergence 74
Applying MACD to Crypto Trading 77

CHAPTER 12: ADVANCED INDICATOR COMBINATIONS 81

Combining Indicators for Better Analysis 81
Customising Indicator Strategies 84

CHAPTER 13: VOLUME ANALYSIS IN THE CRYPTO MARKET 87

Importance of Volume Analysis 87
How to Leverage Volume for Trading 90

CHAPTER 14: CHART PATTERNS FOR CRYPTO SUCCESS 94

Common Crypto Chart Patterns 94
Working with Continuation and Reversal Patterns 98

CHAPTER 15: RISK MANAGEMENT IN CRYPTO TRADING 101

Creating a Risk Management Strategy 101
Tools for Minimising Trading Risks 104

CHAPTER 16: TRADING PSYCHOLOGY: MASTERING YOUR MIND 108

Understanding Trading Psychology 108
Overcoming Emotional Barriers 111

CHAPTER 17: BACKTESTING YOUR CRYPTO STRATEGIES 115

Importance of Backtesting 116
How to Backtest Effectively 118

CHAPTER 18: DEVELOPING YOUR CRYPTO TRADING PLAN 122

Components of a Crypto Trading Plan 123
Customising Your Plan for Success 126

CHAPTER 19: DAY TRADING VS. LONG-TERM INVESTING IN CRYPTO ____ 129

Comparing Day Trading and Long-Term Investing ____ 129
Choosing the Right Approach for You ____ 132

CHAPTER 20: CASE STUDIES OF SUCCESSFUL CRYPTO TRADES ____ 136

Learning from Past Successes ____ 137
Analysing Key Trades for Insight ____ 139

CHAPTER 21: LEVERAGING CRYPTO TRADING BOTS ____ 142

Introduction to Automated Trading ____ 142
Evaluating Trading Bot Options ____ 145

CHAPTER 22: EVALUATING CRYPTO MARKET NEWS AND IMPACT ____ 148

Understanding Market News Influence ____ 148
Distinguishing Between Noise and Valuable Information ____ 151

CHAPTER 23: AVOIDING COMMON CRYPTO TRADING PITFALLS ____ 154

Identifying Common Mistakes ____ 154
Strategies to Avoid Trading Errors ____ 157

CHAPTER 24: BRIDGING THE GAP: TRADITIONAL MARKETS VS. CRYPTO _ 160

Recognising Differences and Similarities ____ 160
Translating Traditional Market Skills to Crypto ____ 163

CHAPTER 25: FUTURE TRENDS IN CRYPTO TRADING ____ 166

Emerging Trends and Technologies ____ 166
Preparing for the Future of Crypto Trading ____ 169

CONCLUSION ____ 173

GLOSSARY OF CRYPTO TRADING TERMS ____ 176

Introduction

In the ever-evolving world of finance, crypto trading has emerged as a revolutionary frontier, capturing the interest and imagination of countless aspiring traders and investors worldwide. Navigating the cryptocurrency landscape requires both an adventurous spirit and a solid analytical foundation. As you embark on this exciting journey, it becomes essential to develop the skills necessary for interpreting market trends, analysing charts, and making informed trading decisions.

This book aims to empower you by bridging the gap between technical knowledge and practical application, ensuring you're well-equipped to tackle the complexities of crypto trading. Drawing from a rich tapestry of strategies and insights, you'll find guidance to boost your confidence as you face the challenges and opportunities presented by the digital currencies market. Our goal is to transform you into a trader who's not just proficient but also adaptable in the face of change.

Crypto trading offers a unique opportunity, yet it demands a keen awareness of the intricacies that lie beneath its surface. Unlike traditional markets, cryptocurrencies are often subject to high volatility, immediate shifts, and unconventional market forces. In order to navigate this dynamic environment successfully, a trader must hone their analytical skills and develop an understanding of both fundamental drivers and technical indicators.

While some might feel overwhelmed by the sheer volume of information, technical analysis serves as a guiding star. It allows traders to interpret price movements, identify patterns, and anticipate future market behaviour based on historical data. This analytical approach provides a coherent framework for evaluating and predicting market trends, enhancing your ability to execute timely and strategic trades.

Within these pages, we'll delve into various analytical tools, complementing your foundational knowledge with advanced techniques designed to maximise your trading potential. Whether you're deciphering candlestick patterns, identifying support and resistance levels, or gauging market sentiment through volume analysis, each concept is crafted to serve as a building block for your trading arsenal.

To complement our analytical journey, we'll explore essential risk management strategies and delve into the psychology of trading. Understanding the emotional landscape of trading is crucial; fear and greed are formidable foes that can derail even the most meticulously crafted plans. By mastering your mindset, you bolster your resilience against the psychological pitfalls that often accompany financial decision-making.

This book is structured to provide a comprehensive roadmap for both beginners and those with some trading experience. The chapters carefully weave together intricate concepts with actionable insights, challenging you to apply your learnings practically and progressively. The knowledge you'll gain is not merely theoretical; it is intended to drive results, optimise performance, and cultivate a profitable trading philosophy.

The rapidly changing crypto market requires that traders be adaptable and constantly learning. New technologies and trading platforms are frequently introduced, offering fresh opportunities yet increasing complexity. This constantly shifting landscape underscores the importance of continuous education and the ability to pivot your strategies to meet current demands. By staying informed about emerging trends, you place yourself ahead of the curve and increase your odds of success.

Throughout this book, emphasis is placed on learning from both successes and failures, encouraging an approach of reflective growth. Case studies and real-world examples are peppered throughout, illustrating key concepts and offering firsthand insights into successful trading strategies applied in diverse market conditions. The aim is to equip you with a tactical edge, ensuring you can apply these lessons when facing live markets.

By providing a thorough understanding and empowering you with the tools of analysis, this book seeks to shape the future of your trading journey. Whether you envisage yourself as a day trader, leveraging short-term movements, or an investor seeking long-term opportunities, the insights provided here are designed to enhance your strategic outlook and trading acumen.

As you turn the pages, imagine the wealth of possibilities that crypto trading holds. Visualise a future where each trade is a calculated decision, backed by insight and executed with precision. The path forward is one of continual discovery, and with the knowledge shared within this book, you will be well-prepared to navigate the exciting terrains of crypto trading.

Welcome to a transformative journey in understanding and mastering the art of crypto trading. Let's illuminate the possibilities, harness the potential, and achieve trading excellence together. The gateway to a new realm of financial exploration beckons, and your journey starts here.

Chapter 1: Understanding the Basics of Crypto Trading

Diving into the world of crypto trading presents both an exhilarating challenge and an educational journey. In an environment where digital currencies redefine the notion of value, aspiring traders must first build a solid foundation in the basics. It's important to understand that crypto trading isn't simply about buying low and selling high; rather, it involves a sophisticated dance involving market trends, investor sentiment, and technological expectations. Establishing a firm grasp of crypto market dynamics and recognising key players within this space can significantly alter your strategies and outcomes. By equipping oneself with the necessary knowledge and tools, crypto traders unlock the potential to turn data-driven insights into successful trading decisions. The journey begins here, laying down the groundwork for your future as a confident and informed participant in the dynamic world of cryptocurrency trading.

Exploring the Crypto Market Landscape

The world of cryptocurrencies is vast and dynamic, offering an exciting frontier for aspiring traders and investors. To truly grasp the essence of crypto trading, it's essential to navigate the unique landscape that this digital asset class presents. Cryptocurrencies, often heralded for their decentralised nature, are fundamentally reshaping financial interactions. Understanding this market landscape involves recognising the factors that fuel its movements, the technological bedrock it stands on, and the myriad opportunities and challenges it brings.

At its core, the crypto market is a network of digitised tokens operating on blockchain technology. These tokens are not just transactional units but often represent projects and technologies that seek to solve real-world problems. The market is open 24/7, a stark contrast to traditional stock exchanges. This constant activity can be invigorating for keen traders, yet it underscores the need for diligent market oversight. Unlike traditional markets, which may have settled patterns that one can depend on through extensive historical data, the crypto market's volatile and unpredictable nature calls for an adaptable mindset and swift decision-making abilities.

Volatility is both an allure and a caution in the crypto market landscape. Prices can surge or plummet at eye-watering speeds, driven by speculative trading, sudden market sentiment shifts, or influential social media posts. This volatility opens doors to significant gains, but it equally poses risks of steep losses. For investors, particularly those fresh to the scene, it's vital to appreciate this duality. Instead of fearing volatility, seasoned traders often embrace it, honing strategies that leverage these fluctuations.

The crypto market doesn't operate in isolation. It's profoundly influenced by external factors, including regulatory developments, economic indicators, and even geopolitical events. Government stances on cryptocurrency legislation can buoy or batter market confidence. As countries seek to harness or curtail these digital assets, staying informed about regulatory trends is crucial for traders. Moreover, news of technological advancements or security breaches can stir or unsettle the market waters. Traders must cultivate an ability to quickly discern which pieces of news bear deep implications and which merely feed market noise.

Blockchain technology, the backbone of most cryptocurrencies, is revolutionary in its transparency and security features. Yet, it remains a double-edged sword. While the trustless nature of blockchain negates the need for intermediaries, the complexity of understanding various blockchain protocols can be daunting. For example, differentiating between blockchain consensus mechanisms like Proof of Work and Proof of Stake can influence an investor's choice of asset. Grasping these technical underpinnings is not just academic but practical, as it empowers traders to assess the long-term viability of crypto assets.

Diving further into the market dynamics, one must consider the diverse array of crypto tokens. While Bitcoin and Ethereum often dominate headlines, they are just the tip of a vast iceberg. Alternative coins or 'altcoins' present a varied landscape where innovative projects attempt to carve niches. Some tokens offer utility on specific platforms, while others might represent a stake in a new kind of digital economy. Discerning investors take time to research and understand potential investments, evaluating them not just on price trends but also on project fundamentals and team strengths.

Engagement in the crypto market also means engaging with its distinctive culture. Crypto enthusiasts, often clustered in online communities, are known for their zeal and community advocacy. Platforms like Reddit, Telegram, and Discord buzz with discussions that can sway perception and momentum. These communities often share insights, though it's crucial to retain a healthy scepticism and independently verify claims before acting upon them. Investing involves balancing subjective sentiments with objective analysis.

The trading strategies that thrive in crypto are as varied as the assets themselves. While some traders prefer fundamental long-term holding, banking on a project's promise, others delve into technical analysis, swiftly transitioning in and out of positions within minutes or hours. This diversity is what makes crypto trading an art as much as a science. Time frames, risk tolerance, and personal financial goals play significant roles in shaping one's approach. Successful traders combine disciplined methodology with intuition honed over time.

Additionally, liquidity is a critical consideration in the market landscape. It refers to how easily one can buy or sell an asset without causing a significant price change. Larger cryptocurrencies like Bitcoin tend to have high liquidity, a factor that traders may rely on for consistency in execution. For altcoins, liquidity can vary widely, potentially adding another layer of complexity to trading decisions. Recognising liquidity conditions helps traders in making informed decisions, ensuring they enter and exit positions under preferable terms.

Amidst all the action, it's also vital to plan strategically for the long-term horizon. While daily or even hourly price swings might tempt shifts in strategy, long-term vision and understanding market cycles can offer valuable anchor points. Veterans of the crypto market often stress the benefit of zooming out, assessing trends over weeks, months, or even years to guide their investment ethos. This perspective assists in weathering temporary storms and capitalising on broader upward trajectories.

The gateway to the world of crypto is understanding its landscape. Aspiring traders are encouraged to keep learning, remain adaptable, and maintain a passion for exploring this ever-evolving market. It is through comprehensive knowledge and strategic application that one can hope to navigate, and indeed thrive, within the captivating crypto market landscape.

Key Players in the Crypto Market

As the crypto market continues to evolve, identifying the key players becomes essential for aspiring traders and investors looking to deepen their understanding. Within this complex ecosystem, several entities and individuals play pivotal roles, influencing price movements, directing trends, and shaping the future landscape of digital currencies. Knowing who these players are and understanding their functions can significantly enhance your trading strategy.

Firstly, let's talk about exchanges, the marketplaces where cryptocurrencies are bought and sold. Exchanges like Binance, Coinbase, and Kraken are where the bulk of trading activity happens. They provide the infrastructure for liquidity, which is a crucial element for any trader. With a variety of trading pairs and different fee structures, exchanges can directly impact your trading experience and profitability. Their role doesn't stop at providing a platform; they also set the rules that govern trading and security, making them essential gatekeepers of the crypto realm.

Further shaping the crypto market are institutional investors, who have stepped in with significant capital. Institutions like Grayscale and MicroStrategy have made substantial investments in cryptocurrencies, particularly Bitcoin, bringing a level of stability and credibility to the market. Their participation tends to be a double-edged sword. On one hand, their presence signals market maturity. On the other, large-scale buy-ins can lead to significant price fluctuations, impacting smaller traders. Aspiring investors should pay close attention to institutional movements as indicators of market sentiment.

Then there are the mining entities, especially relevant in the context of proof-of-work cryptocurrencies such as Bitcoin. Miners play the crucial role of validating transactions and securing the network. Large mining farms, mainly located in regions with low electricity costs, dominate this space. The power they wield can influence the security and operational costs of networks, which can, in turn, impact coin prices indirectly. With ongoing debates about energy consumption, mining operations are at the heart of evolving narratives within the market.

Another significant group is the developers and core contributors of cryptocurrency projects. These technical experts and visionaries are responsible for coding and maintaining blockchain platforms. For example, the Ethereum Foundation includes a global team of developers working tirelessly to improve the Ethereum network. Any updates, forks, or changes proposed by developers can lead to shifts in market opinion and are closely monitored by traders and investors. With significant events like Ethereum's shift from proof-of-work to proof-of-stake, developers' choices can dramatically affect market dynamics.

A separate but equally vital category belongs to the financial analysts and media influencers who interpret and broadcast market trends to the public. These players often shape retail investors' perceptions and decisions. A tweet from a well-known influencer like Elon Musk can cause a coin's price to spike or plummet, emphasizing their power in the market. At the same time, financial analysts offer insights based on data and trends, helping traders make informed decisions. Knowing whose analyses to trust can be a critical edge in trading.

Let's not forget about regulators and policymakers. Their presence is increasingly felt as governments attempt to navigate the often uncharted waters of digital finance. Regulations can either foster growth by offering clarity or stifle innovation through restrictive measures. Traders must stay informed about regulatory developments within their respective jurisdictions. Understanding the implications of policies like the European Union's MiCA Regulation or the U.S. SEC's stance on digital assets can help traders manage risks related to legal compliance.

Venture capital (VC) firms also feature prominently as key players in the crypto market. These firms inject capital into promising blockchain startups and existing projects, fostering innovation and enabling scaling. Their investments are often seen as a vote of confidence in particular technologies or teams, influencing market perceptions and the flow of capital. For the observant trader, tracking where VC money goes can be a potent strategy for anticipating future market movements.

Of course, beneath these institutional figures stands the community of retail investors. This group has, at times, been underestimated but holds considerable power in swaying the market. The collective behaviour of retail traders, often coordinated through platforms like Reddit's r/CryptoCurrency, can lead to phenomena such as the notorious "pump and dump." Their participation underscores the fact that the crypto market is fundamentally democratic, with even small-scale players capable of making waves.

Last but not least, decentralised finance (DeFi) platforms are emerging as formidable actors in the crypto landscape. Offering users the ability to lend, borrow, and trade assets without intermediaries, DeFi is reshaping traditional financial paradigms. Projects like Uniswap and Aave are leading the charge, providing both challenges and opportunities for traders seeking to harness the power of decentralisation. Understanding DeFi ecosystems and their function can open up entirely new trading strategies and prospects.

In conclusion, recognising these key players is essential for any crypto trader aiming to navigate the market successfully. Their interactions create a dynamic environment where fortunes can be made or lost with rapid market shifts. An astute trader will observe, understand, and anticipate the actions of these players, crafting strategies that respond effectively to the ever-changing crypto landscape.

CHAPTER 2: FUNDAMENTAL ANALYSIS FOR CRYPTO

As we delve deeper into the world of cryptocurrency trading, understanding fundamental analysis becomes imperative. It's all about getting to grips with the intrinsic value of a crypto asset, beyond the noise of volatile price swings. This chapter focuses on the various facets of fundamental analysis tailored for the crypto market. Unlike traditional assets, cryptocurrencies are often driven by unique factors such as community support, protocol utility, and innovation potential. Evaluating the strength of a crypto project involves scrutinising whitepapers, analysing the credibility of development teams, and assessing market sentiment. By honing these skills, aspiring traders and investors can distinguish between fleeting digital fads and robust, long-term investment opportunities. The ability to interpret these elements empowers you with the confidence to make informed decisions and strategically position yourself in this dynamic market landscape.

Importance of Crypto Fundamental Analysis

In the vibrant world of cryptocurrencies, where volatility is the norm and markets can quickly sway from euphoria to panic, it's crucial to understand what truly underpins the value of digital assets. Fundamental analysis serves as a guiding light amidst the chaos, helping aspiring traders and investors make informed decisions based on substance rather than speculation. Unlike traditional financial securities, cryptocurrencies often lack the financial history and established metrics that traders have relied on for decades. Here, fundamental analysis steps in to fill the gap, offering a framework to evaluate the intrinsic value of a crypto asset beyond just its market price.

Crypto fundamental analysis encompasses a myriad of factors, each unique to the digital realm. It begins with the basics: understanding the purpose and functionality of a cryptocurrency. Is it merely a digital form of cash, or does it offer something more, like operating as a decentralized platform for applications? Delving into the utility of a crypto asset provides the foundation for assessing its potential for adoption and long-term viability. Projects with well-defined use cases and robust technological frameworks often have a higher chance of sustaining their value over time.

Another crucial component of fundamental analysis in the crypto sphere is examining the project's team and community. The people behind a cryptocurrency can significantly influence its trajectory. Are the founders reputable, with a proven track record in blockchain technology or related fields? A strong team can instil confidence, drawing institutional and retail interest alike. Moreover, an active and engaged community can be a testament to the project's resilience and potential for innovation. Platforms with vibrant ecosystems tend to be more adept at weathering market fluctuations and adapting to ever-evolving industry demands.

Tokenomics, or the economic model of a cryptocurrency, is also a pivotal aspect of fundamental analysis. One must scrutinise how tokens are distributed, their scarcity, and the mechanisms in place to incentivize holding or using them. Inflationary or deflationary characteristics can significantly impact the perceived value of a token. For instance, assets with a capped supply might appeal more to those fearing inflation, while those with a continuous supply model might be leveraged for different utility dynamics. Understanding these aspects can empower investors and traders to gauge potential future movements based on economic incentives embedded within the crypto asset itself.

Moreover, the technological foundations and roadmap of a cryptocurrency can't be ignored. In a domain where innovation is relentless, the underlying technology's robustness and the project's ability to execute its roadmap play a decisive role. A well-defined and executed roadmap suggests a vision and commitment to growth and improvement, which are compelling indicators of a project's potential success. Investors should investigate any upcoming developments, upgrades, or partnerships that might enhance the asset's utility or adoption prospects.

Market dynamics, too, form an essential part of fundamental analysis. Understanding the landscape in which a cryptocurrency operates aids in recognizing competitive threats and opportunities. Competitive analysis helps identify whether a crypto asset has a unique value proposition or if it simply replicates existing offerings. Additionally, macroeconomic factors can influence demand and supply dynamics, and regulatory news can spur or dampen market sentiment significantly.

In considering all these factors, fundamental analysis doesn't exist in isolation from technical or sentiment analysis; rather, it complements them. While technical analysis might highlight how a market is reacting in the short term, fundamental analysis digs deep to understand the why and the potential longevity of those movements. By marrying the two, traders can develop a comprehensive view that encapsulates current market conditions and potential future trajectories.

Successful crypto trading requires not just a keen eye for detail but also the ability to synthesize diverse information sources. Fundamental analysis gears you with this ability, transforming data into insight and, ultimately, into strategy. In a market flooded with enthusiasm and fear, it's the rational, informed trader who often has the edge, poised to navigate fluctuations with confidence.

Lastly, embracing fundamental analysis is an ongoing journey. The crypto environment evolves rapidly, necessitating constant learning and adaptability. Staying updated with developments, continuously reassessing fundamental aspects, and keeping an open mind to new tools and methodologies are vital for succeeding in the dynamic crypto market. As you delve into this intriguing world, fundamental analysis acts as your compass, pointing you towards informed and potentially rewarding investment paths.

Evaluating Crypto Projects and Teams

Understanding what sets a solid crypto project apart from a shaky one is crucial for any discerning investor. When we delve into evaluating crypto projects and teams, we are focused on assessing the true backbone of these digital ventures. At the heart of every promising crypto project lies a dedicated team equipped with vision, technical prowess, and reliability. Evaluating these projects is essential, as it can mean the difference between a successful investment and a financial setback.

The initial step in assessing any crypto project involves a thorough review of its whitepaper. This document is more than just a formality; it illuminates the project's purpose, the problem it aims to solve, and the technology behind it. A readable, transparent, and detailed whitepaper reflects a project that understands its domain and is committed to solving real issues. It should cover topics like the project's utility, underlying technology, tokenomics, and roadmap. If the document seems overly complex or appears to skirt around critical details, it might be a red flag signalling potential issues.

Beyond the whitepaper, it's important to investigate the team behind the project. A project's success heavily relies on the individuals steering it. Look at their track records and experience. Are there familiar names with a history of delivering successful projects? Do they possess the necessary technical skills and industry knowledge? Team members with strong backgrounds in blockchain, finance, or the specific field the project is targeting are preferred. Availability of their profiles, through professional platforms like LinkedIn, adds a layer of legitimacy and transparency.

Moreover, transparency isn't just about names and CVs. Active engagement with the crypto community is a key indicator of a project's viability. Teams that participate openly in forums, AMAs (Ask Me Anything sessions), and social media build trust and offer reassurance of their commitment to the project's success. Are they willing to address queries and criticisms in a forthright manner? Enthusiastic and honest communication can signal a project's long-term sustainability.

While evaluating the team, investors must also consider the project's advisors. These experts lend credibility and offer strategic guidance. Well-known advisors with reputable standing in the crypto sphere could imply robust strategic direction for the project. However, the mere presence of star-studded advisory boards isn't an assurance of success; their active involvement is what truly counts.

The project's strategic partnerships also provide a window into its future potential. Collaborations with established enterprises can enhance credibility and foster growth. Such alliances may increase the utility of the crypto application, extend market reach, and add value to the end users. Evaluating these relationships helps investors understand potential market traction and project timelines.

An often overlooked aspect of evaluation is the legal and regulatory compliance of the project. In an industry frequently scrutinised for its lack of regulation, understanding a project's legal obligations is crucial. Does the project adhere to relevant laws within its jurisdiction? Compliance with international guidelines and obtaining necessary licenses demonstrate a commitment to operating within the law, thus lowering potential risks for investors.

Tokenomics, or the economic model of the cryptocurrency, should align with the project's goals and provide a sustainable future. Examine the structure of the token sale, distribution plans, and incentivisation models. Does the token provide genuine utility, or is it merely speculative? The distribution strategy should ensure that tokens are proportionately allocated to prevent centralisation, which could lead to unfavourable market manipulation.

Community involvement often serves as the pulse of the project. A strong, active community signifies trust and engagement, often acting as advocates for the project. Check online forums, project communities on platforms like Telegram or Reddit, and social media discussions. Communities that are informed, involved, and enthusiastic propel the project forward, sometimes even aiding in troubleshooting and testing phases.

Finally, evaluate the project's competitive landscape. Analyse how it differentiates itself from existing solutions and identifies its unique selling points. The presence of a clearly defined competitive edge or innovation can significantly affect its long-term viability. If a project simply replicates existing solutions without offering any unique attributes or improvements, its potential for success diminishes.

In crypto, due diligence is your most powerful ally. Evaluating crypto projects and teams is a nuanced process requiring attention to detail and critical analysis. Remember, successful trading isn't only about patterns and charts; it's about understanding the core elements that make up a project's foundation. By studying all facets of a project, from the minutiae in whitepapers to broad strategic alliances, you empower yourself with the knowledge to make informed, confident investment decisions.

Chapter 3: Introduction to Technical Analysis

As we journey into the realm of technical analysis, it's vital to appreciate its role as a cornerstone of successful crypto trading. Technical analysis involves examining past market data, mainly price and volume, to anticipate future market behavior. This approach stands distinct from traditional market analysis, offering unique insights tailored to the fast-paced and volatile crypto market. While grappling with price charts might seem daunting at first, the emphasis is on simplifying complex patterns and spotting trends that can significantly impact your trading decisions. By embracing these techniques, you're equipping yourself with a toolkit to make informed predictions and strategic trades. Understanding the nuances of technical analysis empowers you to navigate the crypto market's ebbs and flows with greater confidence and precision, transforming data into actionable insights. As such, this chapter serves as your guide to mastering the art of reading crypto charts, setting the foundation for more advanced topics in the chapters ahead.

What is Technical Analysis?

Technical analysis is a method that aims to forecast future price movements by examining past market data, particularly price and volume. In the realm of crypto trading, understanding technical analysis can empower traders to make informed decisions without solely relying on fundamental aspects such as news or project developments. By analysing charts and identifying patterns, one gains insight into market sentiment and potential price trajectories.

At its core, technical analysis is built on three fundamental assumptions. Firstly, the market discounts everything. This means all relevant information is already reflected in the asset's price, allowing analysts to focus solely on price movements. Secondly, prices move in trends. This assumption highlights that market movements are not random, but follow trends that can be identified and leveraged. Lastly, history tends to repeat itself. Patterns and movements observed in the past are likely to reoccur as market participants behave in similar ways under similar circumstances.

The tools of technical analysis are varied, ranging from simple line charts to complex algorithms. Traders often begin with basic chart types, like line, bar, or candlestick charts, to depict price movements over time. Each chart type offers a different perspective, catering to the analyst's preference or specific trading needs. Learning to interpret these charts effectively is fundamental for any aspiring trader.

Understanding technical analysis requires a grasp of myriad components. One such component is chart patterns, which visually represent the ongoing battle between buyers and sellers. Different patterns suggest potential market movements, and recognising these patterns can provide traders with vital entry and exit signals. For example, patterns such as head and shoulders or double tops and bottoms can indicate reversals, while flags or pennants might suggest continuations of the current trend.

Indicators also form an integral part of technical analysis, with moving averages, relative strength index (RSI), and moving average convergence divergence (MACD) being popular choices. These tools help smooth out price data and create a clearer view of trends and potential reversals. Each indicator offers unique insights, and combining multiple indicators can enhance analytical precision.

A key element of technical analysis is understanding the importance of support and resistance levels. These horizontal lines on a chart indicate where the price has historically struggled to move above (resistance) or below (support). Recognising these levels can help traders anticipate potential price bounces or breakthroughs, thereby crafting more effective strategies.

The application of technical analysis in crypto trading also comes with its own set of challenges. Cryptocurrencies are notoriously volatile, with prices often subject to rapid and significant swings. This volatility can sometimes distort technical patterns and require traders to be extra vigilant. Despite these challenges, the principles of technical analysis remain a valuable tool for navigating the erratic waters of crypto markets.

Moreover, the decentralised nature of cryptocurrencies introduces a unique twist to traditional technical analysis. Unlike stocks or commodities, where market hours define trading periods, crypto markets operate non-stop. This round-the-clock availability means that global events can impact prices at any moment, adding an extra layer of complexity to technical analysis.

The art and science of technical analysis go hand in hand. While the former involves the subjective interpretation of patterns, the latter involves the use of quantitative data to make calculated decisions. The balance between intuition and analysis is what makes technical analysis both challenging and rewarding. As crypto markets evolve and expand, so too does the field of technical analysis, opening up new opportunities for both novice and experienced traders.

Technical analysis is more than just charting; it’s a mindset. By delving deep into price movements and market trends, traders cultivate a disciplined approach to trading. This discipline helps to mitigate emotional decision-making, a common pitfall in crypto trading. Over time, by honing the skills of technical analysis, traders can not only interpret charts with greater accuracy but also develop a resilient trading strategy.

In essence, technical analysis equips traders with the ability to view the market through a lens of patterns and probabilities. It's a powerful tool that transforms raw data into actionable insights. As you embark further into the world of crypto trading, embracing the principles of technical analysis can pave the way to more informed and confident trading decisions.

By continually practicing and refining your technical analysis skills, you're building a foundation that can withstand the unpredictable nature of crypto markets. Remember that expertise is acquired through persistence, curiosity, and a willingness to learn from both successes and setbacks. As you grow in your understanding of technical analysis, you'll be better positioned to seize opportunities and navigate the challenges that lie ahead in your trading journey.

Differences Between Crypto and Traditional Market Analysis

As we delve into the intricacies of technical analysis in the world of finance, it's crucial to acknowledge the distinctive characteristics that define the crypto market compared to traditional financial markets. The first glaring difference stems from the markets' very nature — while traditional markets like stocks and commodities have been around for centuries, cryptocurrencies have only recently emerged. This relative youth means crypto markets are less mature, with unique dynamics driving their movement.

One of the most significant aspects of this disparity is market volatility. Unlike traditional markets, which are generally considered more stable, the crypto market is renowned for its unpredictable and often dramatic price swings. Such volatility can be attributed to several factors, including the market's global nature and the absence of centralised control. While volatile movements can present lucrative opportunities, they also introduce heightened risk, challenging traders to sharpen their strategies in response to rapid changes.

A further factor to consider is the operational hours of these markets. Traditional stock exchanges and commodities markets operate on specific schedules tied to their geographical locations. For instance, the New York Stock Exchange is open from 9:30 AM to 4:00 PM Eastern Time. In contrast, the crypto market operates 24/7, with no closing bell to signal the end of the trading day. This availability can be both a blessing and a curse. While it offers traders increased flexibility, it also necessitates constant vigilance and strategic planning to guard against unexpected price shifts during off-peak hours.

Liquidity, or the ease of buying and selling without causing a significant impact on an asset's price, also differs markedly between these markets. Traditional markets benefit from established liquidity providers and institutional traders, resulting in relatively stable prices and smoother transaction processes. The crypto market, however, often experiences liquidity issues, especially for less-known or new cryptocurrencies. This can lead to increased slippage and wider bid-ask spreads, aspects that traders must navigate carefully when entering or exiting positions.

Additionally, the fundamental actors influencing these markets are distinct. Traditional markets are swayed by institutional investors, hedge funds, and retail traders in an environment regulated by governmental bodies like the Securities and Exchange Commission (SEC) or the Financial Conduct Authority (FCA). These actors and the regulatory frameworks that surround them assure a level of predictability and help mitigate drastic price manipulations. In contrast, the crypto market can be significantly influenced by retail investors, with trends often catalysed by social media hype or influencer endorsements. The regulatory environment is disparate and still evolving, adding another layer of unpredictability.

The role of sentiment analysis also takes on a new dimension in crypto markets. While traditional market analysis often hinges on corporate earnings reports or macroeconomic data such as GDP or employment rates, the crypto realm frequently reacts to developments in technology, security vulnerabilities, and legislative announcements. Crypto traders must, therefore, be adept at interpreting not only traditional news but also real-time updates from crypto projects and blockchain advancements.

Security is another critical area of divergence. Traditional markets operate through regulated, centralised exchanges that typically have robust security measures in place to protect investors' funds. Cryptocurrencies, being generally exchanged on unregulated platforms, introduce additional risks related to hacking and fraud. Ensuring the security of one's holdings involves understanding wallet management, private keys, and the potential risks associated with different exchanges.

Finally, the investment strategies employed in these markets often diverge due to the distinctive characteristics of the assets. While time-tested strategies like technical indicators and chart patterns are applicable to both, crypto traders need to accommodate the rapid technological advancements and shifting fundamentals inherent in cryptocurrencies. For instance, the introduction of new consensus algorithms or forks can drastically alter a cryptocurrency's value, requiring traders to adapt quickly.

The differences between crypto and traditional market analysis are not merely academic; they embody the very challenges and opportunities that traders face daily. Understanding and embracing these differences not only enhances a trader's ability to navigate market complexities but also equips them to harness the unique potential of the crypto realm. As you continue your journey into technical analysis, keep these contrasts in focus. They are the key to crafting strategies that are both resilient and agile in the ever-evolving landscape of cryptocurrency trading.

CHAPTER 4:
READING CRYPTO PRICE CHARTS

Venturing into the world of crypto trading requires more than just a basic understanding—it's about mastering the art of reading price charts to uncover market dynamics. This chapter delves into the essence of crypto price charts, where aspiring traders learn to identify different chart types like line, bar, and candlestick charts. Each chart type tells its own story, revealing the market's sentiment and historical price movements. Equipping yourself with the ability to navigate through various chart features and timeframes is akin to learning a new language; it empowers you to make informed and strategic trading decisions. No longer do charts appear just as lines and bars; they evolve into insightful narratives that guide your trading journey. As you gain confidence in interpreting these visual data spectacles, you stand a greater chance of predicting potential price movements and seizing lucrative opportunities.

Types of Crypto Charts

As you delve deeper into the realm of crypto trading, understanding the various types of charts available to you is crucial. Each chart type offers a unique perspective and serves diverse trading purposes. By mastering these charts, you gain an arsenal of tools to confidently navigate the volatile seas of the crypto market. The most popular chart types include candlestick, line, bar, and Renko charts. Each presents data differently, providing insights that help you spot trends, decipher price movements, and make informed trading decisions.

The most frequently used chart in crypto trading is the **candlestick chart**. Originating from Japan centuries ago, candlestick charts are vibrant with information. These charts display the open, close, high, and low prices of an asset over a designated period. The body of the candlestick either fills with colour to represent a decline or remains unfilled for a rise, giving traders a quick visual snapshot of market sentiment. The "wicks" or "shadows" on either end stretch to show the extremes of price movement within the period, providing insights into market volatility and traders' psychology. By utilising candlestick charts, you can easily spot patterns that signal potential price reversals or continuations, a skill further detailed in later sections.

Then there's the **line chart**, often where many new traders start their journey. Simple yet effective, line charts plot a single point for each period, typically the closing price, and connect them with a line. This offers a streamlined view of the overall price direction and eliminates market "noise" that might obscure the bigger picture. While line charts don't provide the details that candlesticks do, they nonetheless play a critical role in visualising long-term trends and assessing general movements.

The **bar chart** provides more detail than the line chart but without the visual complexity of a candlestick. Also known as the "OHLC" (open, high, low, close) chart, bars represent a period's trading action with vertical lines. These lines show the price range, while small horizontal "ticks" on the sides indicate opening and closing prices. Bar charts can help traders identify strength in a price trend and potential shifts in momentum, making them valuable for spotting opportunities that require immediate attention.

Another intriguing type is the **Renko chart**, derived from the Japanese word for bricks, "renga". Rather than representing time periods, Renko charts focus solely on price movement. A new brick only appears when the price exceeds the specified brick size, entirely disregarding time elapsed. This unique approach filters out minor market fluctuations and highlights more significant shifts, thus clarifying underlying trends. Traders who thrive on longer-term strategies often turn to Renko charts for a clear view of enduring market trends without the distraction of market noise.

In addition to these staples, there are niche charts like **Heikin Ashi** and **Point and Figure** that some traders find invaluable. Heikin Ashi charts smooth out data even further than candlesticks, providing a more coherent view of the trend by averaging price data. With their ability to soften the erratic movements typical in the crypto market, Heikin Ashi charts enhance your capability to discern potential reversals and sustained trends.

On the other hand, Point and Figure charts excel in identifying support and resistance levels, offering a method divergent from time-based charting. These charts focus entirely on price changes and omit the passage of time, resulting in a minimalist expression of market action useful for assessing trend strength and breakout opportunities. This chart type's structured nature demands attention and precision, making it a tool best suited for traders who revel in detail-oriented strategies.

When choosing the right chart type, consider your trading goals and the information you wish to glean from market data. Though each chart type presents data distinctly, their combined use can provide a comprehensive understanding of market conditions. Mastery of multiple chart types enriches your analytical skills and enhances your strategic deployments across different trading scenarios. As you grow more confident, you'll likely find each chart type serves as its own guidepost, illuminating unique aspects of market trends and signalling opportunities in the intricate dance of crypto trading.

In conclusion, developing a robust understanding of these different chart types is indispensable on your journey toward becoming a skilled crypto trader. Utilising the right chart at the right time could be the key difference between a missed opportunity and a fruitful trade. As you continue to explore the vast array of insights each chart offers, you empower yourself to read the stories within the data, paving your way to success in the dynamic world of cryptocurrency trading.

How to Navigate Chart Features

In the realm of crypto trading, the ability to read and interpret charts is like having a compass in the chaotic seas of market price fluctuations. Merely glancing at a crypto chart isn't enough; true mastery involves understanding and navigating its features with precision. Let's embark on this enlightening journey through the intricate landscape of chart features.

The first step in chart navigation is familiarising oneself with the **timeframe** feature. The timeframe represents the granularity of data being displayed. Common timeframes range from one minute to one month. Shorter timeframes like the one-minute or five-minute chart reveal the nitty-gritty of market moves, ideal for day traders who seek to capitalise on brief opportunities. Conversely, longer timeframes like daily or weekly charts offer a broader perspective, essential for those employing swing or position trading strategies. Switching between different timeframes can offer varied insights, revealing both microtrends and macrotrends.

Next, let's delve into the variety of **chart types** available, such as line charts, bar charts, and candlestick charts, each with their distinct utilities. Line charts give a simplified view, connecting closing prices over a period. While they are easy to read, they often miss out on vital data, such as intraday highs and lows. Bar charts fill this gap by showing the open, close, high, and low, bringing more detailed insights. However, it’s the candlestick charts that have captured the imaginations of traders worldwide. They provide a visually intuitive and comprehensive representation of price movements and can depict market sentiment at a glance.

Indicators and overlays are potent tools that can be laid on top of your charts. They serve to enhance a chart's interpretive power. Indicators like moving averages, Bollinger Bands, and various oscillators provide signals for potential trades. Knowing which indicators to employ and when to apply them is an art in itself, often honed by meticulous study and testing. Remember, it's easy to clutter charts with too many indicators, which could create more confusion than clarity. Hence, a minimalist approach, focusing on the most relevant tools, often yields the best results.

You've likely encountered the concept of **support and resistance levels**, which are vital features you'll consistently navigate in charts. These levels indicate price points where markets struggle to move past. Recognising these levels helps traders to set strategic entry and exit points, paving the way for informed decision-making. Drawing horizontal lines along these levels creates a visual cue on the charts, reminding a trader of potential stumbling blocks or launchpads in price action.

Volume bars are another essential feature. Situated typically at the bottom of your chart, they paint a picture of the market's activity level. Volume is an underappreciated ally; it validates trends. A movement with high volume suggests genuine interest and strength, whereas low volume indicates the opposite, signalling potential reversals. By aligning volume trends with price action, traders can gauge the robustness of a trend.

An often-overlooked feature is the **crosshair tool**, a simple yet invaluable tool for data examination. By moving the crosshair along your chart, you can pinpoint exact price points, dates, and corresponding volume data. This precision is crucial when backtesting strategies or comparing historical data to current conditions. Additionally, annotating charts with notes can aid in tracking your thought processes and interpretations over time, serving as a personal guide to past analyses.

Consider the **zoom function** as well, which allows traders to either drill down into the fine details of a specific trading session or to zoom out for a grander overview of market action. Both perspectives are crucial for a well-rounded analysis. This capability can be particularly valuable during periods of volatility or significant market news when examining recent price changes closely

A feature that's straight from the contemporary toolkit is the ability to **set alerts** directly on your charting platform. Alerts can be configured for price movements, trend line breaches, or indicator triggers. These alerts keep you in tune with the market dynamics even when you're away from your trading station. By liberating your time and reducing the need for constant monitoring, alerts provide a seamless trading experience.

For those delving into more advanced charting territory, **drawing tools** like trendlines, Fibonacci retracements, and channels can be integrated into your charts. These tools are not merely decorative; they help elucidate market dynamics and potential future movements. Trendlines can confirm trend direction, while Fibonacci retracements can suggest significant levels where corrections might end. Channels offer a visual means of identifying and confirming trend continuation.

Incorporating **multiple charts** into a single interface is another powerful feature that aids traders in comparing different cryptocurrencies or assets simultaneously. This feature allows a juxtaposition of market movements across different crypto assets, aiding in the identification of correlations and potential arbitrage opportunities.

Learning to **customise and save templates** on your charting platform can significantly streamline your trading routine. With custom templates, you can preserve your preferred setup of indicators, chart types, and drawings just a click away. By doing so, traders save valuable time, which could be better spent conducting deeper analyses or monitoring market changes.

Finally, let's not forget the importance of **staying updated** with the latest features offered by charting platforms. The world of crypto and its accompanying tools evolve rapidly, with regular innovations and upgrades introduced to enhance user experience and charting capabilities. Keeping abreast of these changes ensures you're equipped with the most effective tools for your trading journey.

In conclusion, chart navigation is both an art and a science, demanding patience and practice. The beauty lies in the chart's ability to hold myriad stories and strategies within its axes and lines. Mastering this skill not only amplifies your trading acumen but also empowers you to stride with confidence in the ever-shifting sands of the crypto market.

Chapter 5: Understanding Candlestick Patterns

In the world of crypto trading, candlestick patterns are like a language all their own, offering a snapshot of market sentiment through their visual form. By delving into the basics of these patterns, aspiring traders can begin to understand the underlying emotions driving market trends. Recognising key bullish patterns can signal potential upward momentum, while bearish patterns may warn of impending downturns. Whether it's the strength of a "hammer" or the caution of a "hanging man," each candlestick formation tells a story that helps traders make informed decisions. Mastering these patterns isn't just about memorising formations; it's about developing an instinct that can guide you through the dynamic and often unpredictable crypto markets. As you hone this skill, you'll find yourself more confident in identifying opportunities and crafting strategies grounded in technical analysis.

Basics of Candlestick Patterns

When embarking on the journey of crypto trading, mastering the art of interpreting candlestick patterns can be your compass. These patterns, viewed on a price chart, are a graphical representation of market sentiment. By scrutinizing them, traders can garner insights into the psychology of market participants. At its core, a candlestick pattern can reveal whether bulls or bears hold control over the market for any given period, ultimately aiding in predicting potential price movements.

Each candlestick on a chart tells its own story through four key elements: the open, close, high, and low prices during a specific timeframe. These elements form the body and wicks of the candle. The body is the rectangle created between the opening and closing prices and can be a different colour depending on whether the price closed higher or lower than it opened. Generally, a green or white body signals a price increase, while a red or black body indicates a decrease.

Understanding the nature of these patterns involves not just recognising individual candlesticks but also discerning the broader patterns they create over several candles. For instance, a single bullish engulfing pattern, where a small bearish candle is overshadowed by a larger bullish one that follows, can signify a potential trend reversal from down to up. However, the significance of these patterns is often magnified when they appear at the culmination of a prevailing trend.

Candlestick patterns fall into two main categories: continuation and reversal patterns. Continuation patterns suggest that the current trend is likely to persist. Examples of these include the rising three methods, where small bearish candles follow a larger bullish candle, only to be succeeded by another sizable bullish candle, indicating the continuation of an uptrend.

In stark contrast, reversal patterns hint at a change in the prevailing trend. The hammer and hanging man are prime examples of reversal patterns. Both appear similar but convey vastly different messages depending on their context. A hammer at the bottom of a downtrend hints at a potential reversal upwards, whereas a hanging man at the peak of an uptrend may forewarn a downward reversal.

The significance of candlestick patterns can be substantially enhanced when corroborated by other indicators and signals. It's not uncommon for savvy traders to pair these patterns with moving averages or relative strength index (RSI) signals to validate their assessment. For example, spotting a bullish engulfing pattern near a key support level and alongside an oversold RSI reading might collectively offer a more compelling buy signal.

Moreover, candlestick patterns aren't merely about recognising the shapes but interpreting the story they tell within the larger market context. A doji, a candlestick with a tiny body, often signifies indecision in the market. Its presence at the top of an uptrend could suggest that the bulls' strength is waning, while at the bottom of a downtrend, it might indicate a possible turnaround.

The three black crows and three white soldiers patterns illustrate sequences of consecutive bearish and bullish candles, respectively. Each consecutive candle in these patterns should ideally open within the body of the previous one and close at or beneath/above its close, forming a steady decline or rise that signals strong reversal potential.

To make the most of candlestick patterns in your trading strategy, it's crucial to adopt a disciplined approach. Recognise that not every pattern will lead to a significant market movement; false signals are part of the game. Risk management and a balanced approach should always be kept at the forefront of your strategy, ensuring that only the most promising setups are traded.

Interpreting candlestick patterns is part art, part science. It requires not only knowledge but also practice and keen observation. As you delve deeper into their intricacies, you'll begin to see familiar patterns emerge and recognise them more quickly. This intuitive understanding can become a valuable tool in your trading arsenal.

In conclusion, candlestick patterns form the foundational blocks of understanding price action in crypto trading. While they may seem complex initially, with practice, they offer traders a powerful way to assess market sentiment and predict potential price movements. Remember, success in interpreting these patterns often comes from patience, practice, and the confidence to make informed trading decisions based on combined insights from multiple analytical approaches.

Recognising Key Bullish and Bearish Patterns

Understanding candlestick patterns is a cornerstone of technical analysis. Each candle tells a story of price action and market sentiment, recording buyers' and sellers' battles down to defined time intervals. Spotting key bullish and bearish patterns can empower traders to predict potential price movements. Navigating these patterns with confidence can significantly enhance your trading prowess, offering a beacon amidst the fluctuating tides of the crypto market.

Bullish Patterns mark potential upward reversals. One of the most iconic is the *Bullish Engulfing* pattern. It occurs when a small bearish candle is overshadowed by a larger bullish one, suggesting that bulls have regained control. Traders observe this and anticipate upward movement, presenting them with opportunities to enter or increase positions.

Another prominent bullish pattern, *The Morning Star*, unfolds over three candles, beginning with a long bearish candle, followed by a smaller candle that can be bullish or bearish, and culminating in a potent bullish candle. It signals that the downtrend may be ending, providing traders with a potential entry point.

Further brightening the bullish cadre is the *Piercing Line* pattern, where a long bearish candle is followed by a bullish one that closes more than halfway up the body of the preceding candle. This formation suggests a rebound from a previously bearish sentiment, urging traders to reconsider their bearish outlook.

The presence of a *Three White Soldiers* pattern—comprising three consecutive long bullish candles—is typically a strong bullish signal. This pattern often appears in the aftermath of a downtrend, indicating a powerful comeback for buyers. It's crucial to weigh accompanying volumes and market context, as assumptions based solely on patterns can be risky.

In contrast, **Bearish Patterns** foreshadow potential downward reversals, encouraging traders to consider reducing or hedging positions. The *Bearish Engulfing* pattern mirrors its bullish counterpart. Here, a small bullish candle is enveloped by a larger bearish one, suggesting that sellers have taken the reins.

The Evening Star embodies a bearish counterpart to the Morning Star. It begins with a long bullish candle, followed by a smaller candle, and then a strong bearish candle. This pattern hints at an impending downturn, giving traders a cue to prepare for a potential exit or shorting opportunity.

Another significant bearish pattern is the *Dark Cloud Cover*. It begins with a long bullish candle, followed by a bearish candle that opens above the previous high but closes below the midpoint of the first candle. This pattern indicates a shift to bearish sentiment, often leading traders to expect further bearish developments.

The presence of the *Three Black Crows* pattern—a series of three long bearish candles—is generally interpreted as a robust bearish signal. Appearing after an uptrend, it suggests a strong desire by sellers to drive prices lower. Observant traders will assess additional indicators to confirm this pattern before making decisive moves.

Although mastering these patterns is undeniably beneficial, it's vital to remember that no single pattern tells the entire story. Successful traders learn to combine pattern recognition with other analytical tools, verifying signals through various metrics. This combination enhances accuracy and reduces the chances of falling prey to market noise.

Context remains key. A pattern's significance can vary depending on whether it's observed in a trending or ranging market. Similarly, the strength of the trend might require adjustments to how patterns like the Double Top (bearish) or Double Bottom (bullish) are interpreted. Traders need to remain adaptable and refrain from rigid adherence to textbook patterns.

Emotional discipline also plays a crucial role in trading based on candlestick patterns. Enthusiasm over a perfectly formed pattern may lead to impulsive trades without proper due diligence. Calculated, strategic thinking that aligns with overall trading goals forms the backbone of effective trading decisions.

To conclude this discussion on recognising key bullish and bearish patterns, remember that these patterns are instruments in a trader's larger toolbox. They bolster technical analysis by contributing insights into potential market movements but do require collaboration with broader market perspectives and analysis techniques. By integrating pattern knowledge with a holistic approach, traders can enhance their ability to navigate the dynamic realm of crypto trading, transforming patterns into practical strategies for success.

Chapter 6:

Trend Analysis in Crypto Trading

In the ever-evolving world of crypto trading, mastering trend analysis is akin to wielding a compass in uncharted waters. It's all about understanding the pulse of the market and positioning yourself accordingly. Trends are the underlying currents that drive price movements, and recognising them can make or break a trader's success. By identifying whether a market is trending upwards, downwards, or sideways, traders gain crucial insights into potential entry and exit points. Through effective use of trendlines, trend channels, and moving averages, one can not only interpret price action with more clarity but also increase the probability of executing successful trades. Harnessing these tools isn't just about technical skill; it's about developing an intuitive feel for the rhythm of the market—a skill that, when honed, can inspire confidence and precision in every trading decision.

Identifying Trends in the Crypto Market

In the dynamic world of cryptocurrency trading, the ability to identify trends is an indispensable skill for any trader or investor aiming to make informed decisions. Trends, in essence, reveal where the market has been, where it currently is, and potentially where it is heading. Understanding these patterns can be the difference between a profitable trade and a missed opportunity, providing traders with a roadmap to navigate the volatile crypto markets.

At the heart of trend analysis is the concept of market sentiment, which is the overall attitude of investors towards a particular asset or the market as a whole. Positive sentiment often leads to upward trends, while negative sentiment typically results in downward trends. Recognising these attitudes through price action is what makes trend identification so effective. Think of trends as the heartbeat of the cryptocurrency market – they signal momentum and give traders crucial insights into market dynamics.

Trends in the crypto market can be broadly categorized into three types: uptrends, downtrends, and sideways or horizontal trends. An uptrend is characterized by higher highs and higher lows, indicating that prices are generally on the rise. In contrast, a downtrend consists of lower highs and lower lows, signalling a decline in prices. A sideways trend, meanwhile, occurs when the market moves within a relatively narrow range without establishing a clear direction. Each of these trends offers different opportunities and requires distinct strategies to capitalise on them effectively.

Identifying an uptrend can empower traders to ride the wave of optimism that permeates the market during these periods. A trader recognising an early uptrend can take long positions, aiming to profit from the ascending prices. It's crucial to back such insights with robust analysis, often complemented by other technical indicators, to confirm the trend's strength and sustainability.

Conversely, recognising a downtrend allows traders to prepare for declines by either taking short positions or protecting existing investments. Downtrends can reveal opportunities for those who are skilled in short-selling or for those looking to buy assets at lower prices during subsequent recovery phases. In both cases, the key lies in the trader's ability to accurately determine when a trend is forming and the potential duration before it reverses or stalls.

Sideways trends, on the other hand, present a form of consolidation where the market takes a breather before deciding its next directional move. Traders can exploit sideways trends by engaging in range trading strategies, buying at support levels and selling at resistance. Though less dramatic than their directional counterparts, horizontal trends still present valuable opportunities for traders who understand how to navigate them.

To effectively identify crypto market trends, traders rely on a mix of chart patterns, indicators, and historical data analysis. Chart patterns such as head and shoulders, triangles, and flags can often signify the continuation or reversal of a trend. For those well-versed in interpreting these patterns, they offer critical entry and exit points within the trading cycle.

Complementing chart patterns are technical indicators such as moving averages, RSI, and MACD, which provide more quantitative insights into trends. Moving averages, for instance, can smooth out price data to help traders see the overarching trend direction, offering valuable support in confirming bullish or bearish market conditions. Similarly, the RSI can identify overbought or oversold conditions, suggesting potential trend reversals.

Historical data, too, plays an integral role in trend identification. By studying past market behaviour, traders gain insight into how similar market conditions influenced price movements. While history doesn't always repeat itself, it often rhymes, giving traders a framework to anticipate potential future movements. This, coupled with a comprehensive understanding of current market drivers, allows one to craft a narrative of where the market might be headed.

It's crucial to remember, though, that the crypto market's inherent volatility means trends can be fleeting and susceptible to abrupt changes. External factors such as regulatory news, macroeconomic shifts, or technological advances can disrupt established trends.

Therefore, maintaining flexibility in your analysis and being open to recalibrating your strategy as new data emerges is paramount.

The journey towards mastering trend identification in the crypto market involves continuous learning and adaptation. While tools and strategies are available to support your analysis, experience and instinct also play a crucial role. Deepening your understanding of market psychology and honing your ability to interpret signals accurately will enhance your trading acumen.

Ultimately, recognising trends in crypto markets is about piecing together a puzzle. Each piece—be it a chart pattern, indicator, or piece of historical data—contributes to the broader picture. As you sharpen your skills, you'll find yourself better equipped to anticipate market movements and position yourself advantageously. With persistence and practice, the complex world of trend analysis becomes a powerful ally in your trading journey, helping you move from uncertainty to clarity in the uncharted waters of cryptocurrency trading.

Utilising Trendlines Effectively

In the dynamic realm of crypto trading, trendlines stand as a beacon for traders looking to navigate the tumultuous market waters. While many traders fixate on intricate indicators and complex algorithms, the humble trendline often offers a clarity that's unmatched. It's about separating the signal from the noise, focusing on the broader market direction rather than getting lost in the minutiae. A well-placed trendline can provide guidance on when to enter or exit a trade, essentially marking the path through the digital wilderness that is the crypto market.

To begin with, drawing trendlines isn't about obeying strict rules but rather about interpreting the natural flow of the market. A trendline connects two or more price points and extends them into the future to act as a line of support or resistance. There are two main types: upward trendlines, which are bullish, and downward trendlines, which are bearish. Upward trendlines connect a series of higher lows, reflecting underlying market strength, while downward trendlines connect lower highs, suggesting market weakness. Even in a single day's chart, these lines can speak volumes if you've tuned your trader's ear to listen.

Yet, not every price point matters. Selectivity is crucial. For a trendline to be significant, it needs to connect major price action points rather than every twist and turn. In doing so, it offers a clearer picture of the predominant trend, cutting through volatile price fluctuations that often cloud one's judgment. Aspiring traders should realise that less is often more. By focusing on significant highs and lows, they can draw cleaner, more informative lines that pave the way for sound trading decisions.

One of the greatest advantages of trendlines is their versatility. They can be utilised across varying time frames, from minute-by-minute analyses for day trading to weekly or monthly charts for those with a long-term vision. Consider a trader plotting an upward trendline on a daily chart to track a coin's performance over several weeks. That same trader might simultaneously use shorter time frames to monitor the daily ebbs and flows for potential trade opportunities. This multilevel approach enables traders to stay aligned with their broader strategy while remaining nimble to short-term market shifts.

However, like any tool, trendlines have their limitations and should be used judiciously. Markets don't always adhere to neat, predictable patterns. Trendlines can and do break, often heralding significant changes in market direction. When a trendline fails, it's time to reassess, not ignore—the break itself holds valuable information, indicating either a reversal or a pause in the trend. Being prepared for these eventualities can turn potential pitfalls into opportunities.

Interpreting trendline breaks requires an understanding of other technical analysis elements. A solitary break might suggest a momentary market correction, but when combined with other indicators, such as increased trading volumes or a significant candlestick pattern, it might signal a deeper trend reversal. Aligning trendlines with other analytical tools allows for more informed trading decisions, dramatically improving success rates.

Patience, however, remains a trader's best ally. Automated systems and frantic market environments might tempt one to react impulsively. But successful trendline utilisation leans heavily on patience—waiting for a third point to confirm a trendline, looking for corroborating signals before acting on a trendline breach, and having the discipline to stay within the boundaries that the charts dictate.

Over time, trendlines can give traders a unique perspective—an ongoing narrative that blends past performance with future possibilities. Engaging with them isn't just an analytical exercise but a way to build intuition. This intuition, honed through practice and reinforced by strategy, ultimately offers the confidence that every trader seeks. By focusing on these patterns, traders will not only interpret market sentiment more effectively but carry the confidence to act decisively when the time is right.

Take, for instance, a scenario where a cryptocurrency shows a consistent upward trendline over several months. A breakout through this trendline could be a signal that the trend is losing steam or that market sentiment is shifting. Combining this with other signs—a spike in trading volumes or chatter about the digital asset in online forums—might provide the necessary context for a trader to decide whether to cut losses, secure profits, or even double down if they see potential for a rebound.

Ultimately, mastering the art of using trendlines effectively isn't about predictive perfection. It's about stacking the odds in your favour, creating a framework where technical analysis complements logical judgment. It's in these moments of synthesis, where data meets intuition, that traders often find their stride.

In embracing trendlines, aspiring traders open a gateway not just to understanding market movements but to refining trading strategies that align with both their goals and their risk tolerance. As part of a comprehensive approach to crypto trading, mastering the trendline is one step toward making sense of the seemingly chaotic fluctuations of crypto markets. Each line becomes a guidepost, a marker of where the market's been and where it just might be going, anchored always in the rationale of informed trading and strategic foresight.

Chapter 7: Support and Resistance Levels

In the crypto trading journey, understanding support and resistance levels is akin to deciphering a map's cardinal points. These levels act as invisible markers that indicate potential price points where an asset could halt or reverse its current trend. Support levels are akin to a foundation that an asset's price tends to bounce off, preventing a further decline, whereas resistance levels serve as a ceiling where prices often hesitate before breaking higher. Identifying these levels on charts requires astute observation and practice, involving a mix of historical price data analysis and market sentiment. By mastering support and resistance, aspiring traders can gain insights into price movements and enhance their predictive accuracy, empowering them to make more informed trading decisions and refine their strategies as they delve deeper into market analysis.

Defining Support and Resistance

In the complex world of crypto trading, the concepts of support and resistance serve as fundamental elements for technical analysis. Whether you're just starting out or refining your strategy, understanding these concepts can help interpret market dynamics with greater clarity. These levels act as psychological barriers, where buying and selling pressures often converge, ultimately shaping the price movements of cryptocurrencies. By identifying these thresholds, traders can make more informed decisions.

Support refers to a price level where a downtrend can be expected to pause due to a concentration of demand for buying a crypto asset. As the price declines and approaches this point, the belief is that this is a value level where buyers are likely to enter the market, either to hold or push the price back up. Think of support less as a distinct line and more like a zone. These zones often mirror previous lows or coincide with areas of heavy trading.

Conversely, resistance represents a price level where an uptrend may stall due to an increased desire to sell. As the price rises to this level, traders anticipate it as a favourable point to offload assets, banking their profits. This newfound selling pressure may prevent further price ascent, forming a ceiling of sorts. Again, consider this a zone rather than an absolute line, often reflecting earlier peaks or strong areas of interest.

The interplay between support and resistance is dynamic. When a price surpasses a resistance level, this threshold can flip to become a new support level, and vice versa. This phenomenon is known as support-resistance inversion, indicating that a market attitude has shifted. Traders keen to catch these flips gain a tactical advantage by recognising turning points in buyer-seller sentiment.

Identifying these levels requires both art and science. Technical analysts employ various tools and techniques to map them out effectively. By drawing horizontal lines at previous highs and lows, or using Fibonacci retracement levels, traders can visually identify potential support and resistance zones. The key, however, is practice and experience, as the market breathes life into these formations and refines their accuracy over time.

The power of support and resistance lies in their application across different time frames. Short-term traders may look for minute-by-minute fluctuations, while long-term investors may focus on larger trends spanning weeks or even months. This multiscale applicability allows for diverse strategies, catering to varied risk appetites and investment timelines. By accurately predicting these levels, traders position themselves to ride on bullish uptrends or safeguard against bearish declines.

Beyond technical charts, support and resistance levels are steeped in the psychology of market participants. When these levels are repeatedly tested and hold firm, they reinforce market confidence in these barriers. As more traders observe these formations, they tend to act in ways that confirm their validity, creating a self-fulfilling prophecy. Understanding the psychology that drives market participants at these levels can enhance a trader's ability to preempt market reactions.

Despite their importance, relying on support and resistance alone can be risky. The crypto market, known for its volatility, can be unpredictable. Price manipulations and sudden news can cause breaches of these levels. Therefore, adept traders often complement this analysis with other indicators, such as moving averages or trend analysis, to ensure they aren't making decisions in isolation. This multi-faceted approach provides a more comprehensive understanding of the market landscape.

Technology plays a pivotal role in helping traders harness the power of these levels. With advanced charting software and analytical tools, traders can draw, refine, and track support and resistance more accurately than ever before. For the modern trader, this technological edge can spell the difference between capitalising on a critical level and missing an opportunity.

In summary, support and resistance levels are indispensable tools for any crypto trader. These psychological barriers not only aid in anticipating likely price movements but also in understanding the market sentiment. By integrating this understanding with a robust strategy, traders are better placed to navigate the undulating tides of the crypto world with confidence and precision. The path to mastery lies in continuous learning, adaptation, and the judicious application of these principles.

How to Identify Support and Resistance on Charts

Diving into the world of crypto trading can feel like exploring uncharted waters. Here, the concepts of support and resistance serve as your reliable compass, guiding you through turbulent market conditions. Support and resistance levels represent pivotal points on a price chart, indicating the zones where prices historically stop and reverse direction. They hold significant importance for any aspiring trader looking to make informed decisions.

To identify these levels, begin by spotting visible peaks and troughs on your charts. A support level is generally found at a low point, where the price tends to halt its decline and possibly bounce back up. Conversely, resistance levels are where the price typically stops climbing, unable to surpass a certain point. Both support and resistance zones act like barriers, and understanding them is crucial for anticipating future price movements.

Traders often use horizontal lines to demarcate these levels on their charts. When a support or resistance level is tested multiple times without being significantly breached, it strengthens the credibility of that level. To draw these lines effectively, look for areas on the chart where price action has repeatedly reversed. These historical touchpoints often have tales to tell about potential future behaviour.

It's essential to remember that support and resistance aren't exact numbers. They function more as zones or areas with potential for price fluctuation. This understanding can help you avoid the pitfall of assuming a single price point will serve as an absolute stopping point. Instead, monitor how prices react within these zones to gauge possible future movements.

The concept of psychology plays a pivotal role here. Market participants often react to past price levels based on cognitive biases. If a particular price level has held as a support or resistance before, traders may act similarly in future scenarios, creating self-fulfilling prophecies that reinforce these levels.

Using multiple timeframes can enrich your analysis of support and resistance. Short-term charts might highlight minor levels that aren't apparent on a longer timeframe, providing different perspectives on possible price reactions. This multi-layered approach can offer valuable insight, empowering you to make more nuanced trading decisions.

One effective method for identifying these levels involves using moving averages, which we'll explore further in later chapters. Moving averages can act as dynamic support and resistance zones, providing guidance in a market filled with uncertainty. As the average changes, it gives you a moving target to monitor and adapt to.

Additionally, techniques such as Fibonacci retracement levels, pivot points, and trendlines can help in spotting support and resistance. While each of these tools has its unique application, they collectively enrich your ability to identify potential zones of interest, making them indispensable in your trading toolkit.

Armed with this understanding, it becomes possible to anticipate potential reversals or continuations with greater accuracy. For instance, if the price repeatedly tests a support level without breaking, it might suggest a buying opportunity. Alternatively, recognising a strong resistance level could indicate a moment to sell or short-sell an asset.

Understanding that breakthroughs can turn support into resistance and vice versa is also critical. This phenomenon is often referred to as a "flip." In situations where a price breaks through a resistance level and sustains above it, the former resistance can then act as a new support level. By paying attention to these flips, you'll better navigate shifting market landscapes.

It's equally important to complement these insights with market volume analysis. A breakout accompanied by high volume tends to indicate a stronger conviction in the price move, making such moves more reliable than those with low volume. A volume spike at support or resistance levels can be a tell-tale sign that many eyes are watching and reacting, thus validating the current market direction.

In conclusion, identifying support and resistance levels isn't just about drawing lines on a chart. It's an art rooted in market psychology, with layers of technical tools enhancing its precision. By honing this skill, you'll unlock the potential to predict price movements more accurately and bolster your trading strategy with confidence. This foundational understanding serves as your gateway to mastering the nuanced dance of market forces on the crypto stage.

Chapter 8:
Moving Averages and Their Uses

As we delve into the world of moving averages, their ability to smooth out price data and reveal market trends becomes evident, making them a cornerstone tool for crypto traders. Unlike jumping on every short-term price fluctuation, moving averages help traders adopt a more strategic approach by providing clarity amid market noise. They're built on different time frames and can be simple or exponential, each offering unique insights. The simple moving average (SMA) takes a straightforward approach by calculating the average of past prices over a set period, while the exponential moving average (EMA) gives more weight to recent prices, reacting faster to price changes. Implementing these tools with other analyses can transform your trading strategy, guiding you in making informed decisions and refining your entry and exit points. Making moving averages an integral part of your trading toolkit could empower you with enhanced market insight and drive successful trading outcomes.

Types of Moving Averages in Crypto

When navigating the volatile waters of crypto trading, moving averages stand as one of the most reliable tools. They bring a semblance of order to what often seems like chaos. A moving average smooths out the noise of short-term price fluctuations, giving you a clearer picture of the overall trend. But not all moving averages are created equal. Different types come with distinct characteristics and benefits, offering diverse insights into market behaviour.

Let's start with the simplest form, the **Simple Moving Average (SMA)**. This is calculated by averaging a set number of past data points. For instance, a 10-day SMA would sum up the closing prices of the last ten days and divide by ten. The simplicity is in its strengths and weaknesses—it's easy to calculate and understand but treats each price point equally, which might dilute the impact of more recent market dynamics.

In contrast, the **Exponential Moving Average (EMA)** addresses this by giving more weight to recent prices, making it more reactive to the latest market conditions. This is particularly useful in the fast-moving crypto market, where being in tune with the most recent price shifts can mean the difference between catching a trend early and getting left behind. The EMA is favoured by traders looking to capture short-term volatility without wholly forgoing the long-term trend.

Another interesting variant is the **Weighted Moving Average (WMA)**. Much like the EMA, the WMA assigns greater significance to recent prices. However, it does so linearly rather than exponentially. This gives it a slightly different feel, and some traders find it offers a smoother transition in recognising trend changes. In crypto trading, where swift and dramatic shifts are the norm, having an additional measure can be invaluable.

For those focused on reducing lag while still smoothing out volatility, the **Smoothed Moving Average (SMMA)** might be the right choice. Unlike the simpler SMAs, the SMMA incorporates a larger dataset and modifies it gradually, offering insights that are less susceptible to sudden market swings. By doing so, it provides a more stable view, which can be particularly advantageous in markets known for erratic movements like crypto.

Moving averages also pair with each other to form powerful trading signals, such as the **Moving Average Crossover**. This method uses two moving averages—typically an SMA and an EMA set to different periods. Traders watch for the point where the shorter-term moving average crosses above or below the longer-term average, signalling potential buy or sell opportunities. This strategy can be an integral part of a trader's toolkit, especially when aiming to confirm emerging trends.

Additionally, the concept of **Adaptive Moving Averages**, like the Kaufman Adaptive Moving Average (KAMA), offers a dynamic approach to trend identification. It adapts to market conditions by adjusting its weighting factor based on volatility. This makes KAMA exceptionally appealing to traders seeking a moving average that can keep pace with the rapid movements in the crypto sphere without flipping erratically.

It's pivotal to remember that while moving averages provide invaluable insights, they aren't foolproof. The **lag** inherent in these indicators means they sometimes react to events after the fact. In the world of crypto, where opportunities can manifest and vanish quickly, traders must supplement moving averages with other tools and analyses for optimal effectiveness.

Moving averages are versatile and can be customised by adjusting the time period, which further changes their sensitivity and suitability for different trading styles. Shorter periods tend to pick up quick trends, excellent for day traders, while longer periods are ideal for those with a more long-term outlook. This flexibility is crucial for adapting strategies to various market conditions.

Harnessing the power of differing types of moving averages allows traders to form a more comprehensive market view. They act as a compass in navigating the ever-shifting tides of the crypto world. By integrating multiple moving average types, alongside other technical tools, traders can enhance the robustness of their strategies and their ability to predict trends more accurately.

In conclusion, moving averages are more than just lines on a chart—they're a window into the market's mood. Understanding their nuances and the context of their application can transform how traders perceive and interact with the crypto world. Mastery of these tools doesn't just illuminate past trends but lights the way forward, empowering traders to make decisions with greater confidence and clarity.

Implementing Moving Averages in Your Strategy

In the dynamic and often volatile arena of crypto trading, moving averages serve as a foundational tool, offering clarity amidst the chaotic waves of market fluctuations. Once you've grasped the different types of moving averages, incorporating them into your trading strategy can significantly enhance your decision-making process. Understanding how to implement these tools requires both technical knowledge and practical application, acting as a bridge between theory and real-world trading scenarios. Let's delve into how you can effectively implement moving averages in your trading strategy.

When discussing moving averages, it's important to recognise their principal function: identifying the direction and momentum of the market. In crypto trading, where price changes can be sudden and pronounced, moving averages help smooth out price data, creating a more refined visualisation of trends. The two most popular types of moving averages are the simple moving average (SMA) and the exponential moving average (EMA). These tools help traders discern potential signals for entering or exiting positions based on market movements. Knowing which to use—and when—depends significantly on your trading objectives and the characteristics of the specific cryptocurrency you are dealing with.

The simple moving average, by virtue of its straightforward methodology, can be remarkably effective for traders looking to establish the general direction in which a particular cryptocurrency is heading. By providing an average of a coin's price over a specific period, the SMA helps reduce the noise of day-to-day price fluctuations. This characteristic makes it particularly useful for long-term trend analyses. On the other hand, the exponential moving average gives more weight to the most recent prices, making it more responsive to recent market changes. This responsiveness is advantageous for traders aiming to capitalise on short-term movements or those who are engaged in day trading. Thus, understanding the properties and differences of these averages allows for their strategic incorporation into your trading approach.

To effectively implement moving averages, it's crucial to determine the right time frames that align with your trading strategy. A short-term trader might find a 10-day EMA more beneficial for capturing quick price swings, whereas a long-term investor might prefer a 50-day or even a 200-day SMA to understand the broader picture. The ability to adjust the length of the moving average in accordance with your investment horizon is a powerful feature that can be customised to fit your trading style.

Trading signals derived from moving averages are pivotal in formulating entry and exit strategies. For instance, a crossover strategy is commonly employed by traders to identify buy or sell signals. A bullish crossover occurs when a shorter-term moving average crosses above a longer-term moving average, indicating an upward trend and a potential buy signal. Conversely, a bearish crossover, where the shorter moving average slips below the longer one, suggests a downtrend and a potential sell signal. By backtesting these crossovers on historical data, you can determine the feasibility and risk-reward ratio before deploying them in live trading scenarios.

Moreover, integrating moving averages with other technical indicators can enhance their predictive power, making them part of a multifaceted trading strategy. For example, combining moving averages with indicators like the Relative Strength Index (RSI) or the Moving Average Convergence Divergence (MACD) can provide a more comprehensive view of market conditions. This combination offers a confluence of signals that can increase the reliability and accuracy of your trading decisions, reducing the likelihood of false signals.

In addition to using moving averages as standalone signals, they can also serve as dynamic support and resistance levels. In a bullish market, a moving average may act as a support level, where the price tends to bounce off, providing opportunities to enter long positions. In a bearish market, it can function as a resistance level. Recognising these patterns can aid in setting stop-loss orders and profit targets, ensuring that you maintain a balance between risk and reward.

Risk management is another critical aspect where moving averages can play a role. By identifying trend reversals early using moving averages, you can adjust your stop-loss levels and position sizes accordingly, safeguarding against adverse market movements. Implementing a disciplined approach that involves regularly reviewing the signals generated by moving averages can keep you aligned with market trends and mitigate potential losses.

Finally, the psychological aspect of implementing moving averages shouldn’t be overlooked. Confidence in your trading decisions often stems from understanding and trusting the tools you use. By mastering moving averages, you not only enhance your technical analysis skills but also gain an edge in managing the emotional challenges inherent in crypto trading. This assurance enables you to act decisively, fostering a proactive rather than reactive trading mindset.

In conclusion, integrating moving averages into your trading strategy requires a blend of technical understanding, strategic planning, and emotional discipline. By adapting these tools to align with your trading objectives, conducting thorough backtesting, and combining them with other indicators, you can harness their full potential. As you refine your skills and build confidence in your analysis, moving averages will become an indispensable part of your crypto trading toolkit, guiding you through the tumultuous yet rewarding landscape of digital currency trading.

Chapter 9: Crypto Indicators You Need to Know

Venturing into the world of crypto trading becomes significantly more manageable when equipped with the right tools, and understanding key crypto indicators is one such essential tool. These indicators act as compass points, guiding traders through the sometimes turbulent seas of the crypto market by offering insights into potential market directions and shifts. While the sheer number of indicators might seem intimidating, selecting the right ones can be a game-changer in crafting effective strategies. Indicators such as the Moving Average (covered in a previous chapter) provide clarity in detecting trends, but there's an entire arsenal beyond that which can illuminate your trading path. From momentum indicators that gauge the speed and strength of price movements, to volatility indicators that capture price fluctuations, each serves a unique purpose. Deciphering which indicator aligns best with your specific trading goals and market perspective is crucial. Mastering these tools not only helps in making informed decisions but also empowers you to turn data into actionable insights, bolstering confidence in your trading pursuits. This chapter will introduce you to the must-know indicators, encouraging a deeper dive into those that resonate most with your trading style.

Introduction to Crypto Trading Indicators

In the constantly evolving world of cryptocurrency trading, understanding crypto trading indicators is crucial for aspiring traders. These indicators act like navigational tools in the complex waters of the crypto market, helping traders discern patterns, predict price movements, and make informed decisions. While at first they might seem daunting, with time and practice, they become invaluable assets in a trader's toolkit.

Crypto trading indicators are the mathematical computations based on the price, volume, or open interest of a digital asset. They serve to predict future market behaviour by analysing past market data—a concept deeply rooted in the philosophy of technical analysis. This mathematical nature of indicators is crafted into visual forms to help traders easily comprehend market signals and benchmarks.

While the sheer number of indicators available could be overwhelming, it's essential to grasp the fundamental purpose each serves. Broadly, indicators can be categorised into leading and lagging types. Leading indicators, such as the Relative Strength Index (RSI), are designed to predict future price movements, providing traders with signals before the new trend or reversal begins. Lagging indicators like moving averages confirm established trends, giving traders the assurance to continue with an ongoing position.

A common indicator that many traders rely on is the Moving Average Convergence Divergence (MACD), which combines several datasets to generate insights about momentum and trend. Knowing how to employ such indicators efficiently can level the playing field, empowering traders to anticipate changes rather than simply reacting to them. Likewise, the Bollinger Bands, which offer a range of statistical highs and lows, help traders understand market volatility and potential entry or exit points.

Yet, no single indicator can offer foolproof strategies. Much like a craftsman with a diverse toolset, successful traders combine multiple indicators to create a nuanced understanding of market movements. The synergy between indicators can provide a more comprehensive picture, mitigating risks and enhancing prediction accuracy. But keep in mind, relying on too many at once could lead to contradictory signals and analysis paralysis.

Part of mastering crypto trading indicators lies in understanding the specific context of the cryptocurrency being traded. Different assets might exhibit unique behaviours due to their inherent volatility, trading volume, or market perception. A new, highly speculative coin might behave differently compared to more established cryptocurrencies like Bitcoin or Ethereum, which exhibit more predictable patterns.

Adapting to the specific nuances of the crypto market is key. Traditional market indicators such as moving averages, RSI, and MACD still provide valuable insights but tweaking their parameters according to the crypto's characteristics could yield even more accurate results. For instance, adjusting the period of a moving average to fit crypto's often erratic price behaviour could provide more relevant insights.

Implementing crypto trading indicators effectively also demands an awareness of one’s trading goals and risk tolerance. Are you a day trader seeking short-term gains, or are you looking to invest over a longer horizon? The choice of indicators might vary significantly based on strategic objectives. A day trader might focus on short-term volatility indicators, while long-term investors might rely more on trend-following indicators.

In addition to technical knowledge, ethos plays a pivotal role. Successful traders cultivate a mindset that balances patience, discipline, and continuous learning. It's essential to remain sceptical about signals and not fall into the trap of confirmation bias, where one only notices information that confirms pre-existing beliefs while ignoring data to the contrary.

Finally, embracing a dynamic learning process is invaluable. Crypto markets evolve swiftly, influenced by technology, regulation, and macroeconomic factors. As indicators themselves are periodically updated to incorporate newer datasets or technological advancements, staying abreast of these changes ensures that traders aren't left behind. Engaging in communities, participating in webinars, and continuously testing and retuning indicator strategies can offer tangible benefits to one's trading prowess.

Choosing the Right Indicators for Your Analysis

Diving into the world of crypto trading indicators can be both thrilling and daunting. These tools are like the compass on your crypto journey, guiding decisions and helping unveil market trends. With countless indicators at your fingertips, the key question becomes: which ones will best serve your analytical needs?

Begin by understanding the nature of your trading goals. Are you an aggressive trader seeking short-term price movements or a patient investor focusing on long-term market trends? Your approach significantly influences the choice of indicators. For instance, day traders might lean towards momentum indicators such as the Relative Strength Index (RSI) for its ability to capture rapid price fluctuations, whereas those with a long-term focus might consider moving averages to identify persistent trends.

Next, consider the complexity level you're comfortable with. Some indicators are straightforward, like the Moving Average, with its primary job to smoothen price data. Others, like the Moving Average Convergence Divergence (MACD), require a deeper understanding of their components and interpretation.

Beginners should start with simple indicators, gradually building up to more intricate ones as their confidence grows.

Another crucial factor is the type of market conditions. Markets don't remain static; they oscillate between trending and ranging phases. For trending markets, Moving Averages and MACD can illuminate the bigger picture, revealing the strength and direction of a trend. On the flip side, in a ranging market, oscillators such as RSI or Stochastic are often more effective, highlighting overbought or oversold conditions that could precede reversals.

Correlation doesn't equal causation—this axiom holds true in technical analysis. Over-reliance on a single indicator can be misleading. Each indicator offers a specific vantage point, highlighting one or two market aspects. Combining various indicators can provide a more rounded view, minimizing the risk of false signals. However, avoid the common pitfall of indicator overload, which can lead to analysis paralysis. A carefully curated selection of complementary indicators often serves better than a plethora of disconnected ones.

The time frame is yet another consideration when choosing the right indicators. Different indicators perform differently across various time frames. For instance, while a short-term moving average might cater to intra-day analysis, a long-term moving average might offer better insights for weekly or monthly price movements. Align the indicators' time frame with your trading horizon to enhance their effectiveness.

Customisation and adaptation are part of refining your strategy. Don't hesitate to tweak an indicator's parameters to align with your trading style. Most trading platforms allow adjustments to settings, which can be crucial, especially when an indicator's default setting isn't delivering expected insights. Experiment with different settings, backtest them extensively, and find what resonates with your strategy.

It is also invaluable to stay informed about the indicators popular within the crypto community. Platforms like TradingView host a vibrant community of traders sharing insights and configurations that could inspire your approach. Engaging with this community can shed light on market sentiment, popular strategies, and emerging indicator uses.

Ultimately, the right indicators are those that align with your market philosophy and personal trading style. Trust your instincts, backed by data-driven insights that clarify your path. With practise and experience, your choice of indicators will become second nature—akin to an artist with their palette, meticulously crafting each stroke to capture the market's essence.

In this vibrant world of crypto trading, your toolkit shouldn't remain static. Stay inquisitive and adaptive, recognising that the markets evolve and so should your techniques. By continually refining your indicator selection and application, you set the stage to not only read the markets but to understand them more intimately. This way, you can confidently manoeuvre through the crypto tides, turning analysis into successful trading opportunities.

CHAPTER 10:
THE RSI AND ITS APPLICATION

The Relative Strength Index (RSI), a powerful momentum oscillator, offers traders a unique insight into market conditions by measuring the speed and change of price movements. By pinpointing overbought or oversold conditions, the RSI can significantly enhance decision-making processes. Imagine standing at a crossroads, where past price movements are your guide: the RSI helps illuminate the path with its numerical scale from 0 to 100, often spotlighting pivotal trading opportunities. While numbers above 70 may indicate an overbought market, suggesting a potential pullback, readings below 30 hint at oversold conditions ripe for a reversal. Yet, seasoned traders know it's not just about the numbers; it's about reading the broader context—divergence between price action and RSI trends can signal an impending shift. As aspiring traders, understanding how to wield the RSI effectively can transform your analytical toolkit, marrying technical insight with strategic execution, and galvanizing your trading journey with confidence and clarity.

Using RSI for Crypto Trading Decisions

The Relative Strength Index (RSI) is a robust tool for crypto traders, helping them make more informed decisions in the volatile cryptocurrency market. At its core, RSI is a momentum oscillator, measuring the speed and change of price movements within a specific time frame. Traders use it to assess whether a particular crypto asset is overbought or oversold, offering a glimpse into potential reversal points. Grasping how RSI functions in the crypto sphere can significantly enhance your trading strategy.

One of the primary strengths of RSI is its simplicity and the clarity it brings to chart analysis. When applied correctly, RSI can act as a powerful signal for entry and exit points during trading. To illustrate, an RSI value over 70 typically indicates that an asset might be overbought, suggesting that a price drop could be on the horizon. Conversely, a value below 30 may point to an oversold condition, hinting at a potential upward price correction. These indications are not guarantees but serve as alerts to pay closer attention to market trends.

Traders often combine RSI with other indicators to bolster their strategy. For instance, coupling RSI with moving averages or Bollinger Bands can create a more comprehensive view of market conditions. By doing so, you mitigate the risk of acting on false signals, as RSI values could vary depending on market sentiment and external factors, especially in the unpredictable landscape of cryptocurrencies.

RSI also excels in trend analysis. In a bullish trend, RSI tends to remain in the 40-90 range with the 40-50 zone acting as support. Likewise, in a bearish trend, RSI typically stays between 10-60, with the 50-60 zone functioning as resistance. These ranges aid in identifying and validating trends, allowing traders to maintain positions aligned with the prevailing market direction. Understanding how these ranges play out during varying market cycles is crucial to mastering RSI.

Beyond deciphering overbought and oversold levels, RSI can signal trend reversals through divergences. A divergence occurs when the price action of the asset differs from the RSI indicator. A bullish divergence happens when the crypto asset's price makes a lower low, while the RSI forms a higher low. This divergence can hint at a potential reversal to the upside. In contrast, a bearish divergence arises when a higher high in the price coincides with a lower high in RSI, which might precede a downside reversal. Spotting these divergences requires a keen eye, but it's a skill that can lead to profitable trading decisions.

Nevertheless, relying solely on RSI without considering broader market conditions can lead to pitfalls. Cryptocurrency markets are highly susceptible to sudden swings caused by external factors such as regulatory changes, technological advancements, or socio-economic shifts. Therefore, integrating RSI insights with thorough fundamental analysis is crucial — assessing the underlying project, team credibility, and market moves offers a fuller picture.

Adapting RSI periods is another approach traders use to tailor their analysis. The default period is 14, but traders may adjust this setting based on their trading strategy or market condition expectations. Shortening the RSI period makes it more sensitive to price changes but could increase noise, whereas a longer period provides smoother results but might lag in identifying immediate opportunities. Experimenting with different settings can reveal insights specific to your trading style and the cryptocurrencies you're targeting.

Another factor to consider is that different cryptocurrencies might respond differently to RSI signals, influenced by their unique liquidity levels and market capitalisation. As such, regularly backtesting RSI strategies against historical data can offer insights into their effectiveness on specific coins. This process of backtesting can uncover patterns and outcomes, guiding traders in refining their methods to maximise returns.

Emotional control is a vital component when interpreting RSI signals. It's easy to get swayed by rapid RSI movements, especially during high volatility. However, traders should approach RSI indicators with a level-headed perspective, backed by their trading plan and risk management strategy. It's important to remember that while RSI is a valuable tool, it remains an indicator of probability, not certainty.

Inspirational success stories abound within the crypto trading world, where traders have effectively harnessed RSI as part of their analytic arsenal. Yet, these successes are often underpinned by discipline, constant learning, and adaptability. As markets evolve, so should your approach to leveraging RSI. Whether you're navigating a bull or bear market, fortifying your technical analysis skills will keep you poised to seize the next opportunity with confidence.

Ultimately, mastering RSI is about understanding its signals, adapting them to the crypto environment, and integrating them strategically into your trading routine. With practice and patience, RSI can be a guiding beacon, illuminating paths to trading success in the dynamic world of cryptocurrencies.

Chapter 11: MACD: A Powerful Indicator

The Moving Average Convergence Divergence (MACD) is an essential tool in the trader's arsenal that unravels potential buy and sell points through its unique blend of trend-following and momentum. At its core, MACD is crafted by subtracting a longer-term exponential moving average (EMA) from a shorter-term one, creating a flexible oscillator that adapts to varying market conditions. This indicator isn't just about identifying trend direction; it also dynamically reflects the speed and momentum behind price movements, offering a dual perspective that many traders find invaluable. Using the signal line, a third EMA, MACD generates crossover points which suggest potential market entry and exit opportunities. By diving deep into the world of MACD, you equip yourself with the ability to fine-tune trading strategies, ultimately sharpening your edge in the crypto market. As we progress, remember that understanding MACD's signals and intricacies could be a stepping stone to mastering the ever-shifting tides of digital currencies.

Understanding the Moving Average Convergence Divergence

The Moving Average Convergence Divergence (MACD) stands as a beacon for traders deciphering the complexities of crypto market charts. At first glance, this indicator may look like a set of mysterious lines moving up and down, but, with a deeper understanding, it unleashes an array of insights into market momentum. It's a tool that, once mastered, can provide the confidence to make more informed trading decisions.

MACD might be seen as just another acronym in the vast sea of trading jargon, but it holds a profound significance. At its core, the MACD reflects the interplay between two moving averages of a crypto asset's price, shedding light on its momentum and potential direction shifts. Created by Gerald Appel in the late 1970s, MACD has endured through decades of market evolution, continuously proving its worth across different trading environments. Understanding its components is the first step towards mastering its application.

The MACD comprises three critical components: the MACD line, the signal line, and the histogram. The MACD line is the difference between two exponential moving averages (EMAs)—commonly the 12-day and 26-day EMAs. The signal line, typically a 9-day EMA of the MACD line, serves as a smooth reference. The histogram, which represents the difference between the MACD line and the signal line, visually conveys the speed of price movements. This trio dances across the chart, with their interactions signalling potential buying or selling opportunities.

As aspiring crypto traders, grasping how these lines interact isn't just academic; it's a practical necessity. The MACD line crossing above the signal line can indicate that it's time to buy. Conversely, when the MACD crosses below the signal line, it could signal a selling opportunity. Importantly, these crossovers are more significant when they occur at extreme points of the MACD histogram, escalating the urgency of the signals. The distance between the MACD line and the signal line, as depicted by the histogram, suggests the strength of a trend. Longer bars imply stronger trends, while shrinking ones could point towards a weakening momentum.

The MACD isn't infallible—no indicator is. However, when used as part of a broad analytical approach, it strengthens the trader's ability to navigate volatile crypto markets. It's crucial to note that the MACD works best in trending markets. In sideways or non-trending markets, it might generate false signals. Therefore, it's wise to couple MACD with other technical analysis tools, enhancing its effectiveness while minimising misleading signals.

Another potent feature of the MACD is the divergence signal. Divergence occurs when the price of a crypto asset is making a new high or low that isn't confirmed by the MACD. A bullish divergence happens when the price hits a lower low while the MACD achieves a higher low. This scenario might anticipate a price reversal to the upside. Conversely, a bearish divergence forms when prices reach a higher high as the MACD records a lower high, perhaps indicating an impending downturn. These divergences can be powerful predictors of future price movements.

To maximise the MACD's potential, it's essential to consider its settings, which can be adjusted based on a trader's strategy. While the standard 12-26-9 settings are popular, some traders customise their MACD settings to better align with different time frames or specific market conditions. Experimentation and backtesting with varied settings can yield insights into which configuration best complements your trading style.

Trade strategy and charting go hand in hand, and the MACD's versatility makes it integral to various strategies. For instance, in a trending market, traders might rely heavily on MACD crossovers in combination with moving averages to identify entry and exit points. Meanwhile, for those focusing on breakouts, the MACD can confirm the strength of a breakout move when aligned with volume analysis and support/resistance levels. Such strategic applications, forged in the furnace of real-world trading, empower traders to harness the MACD's full capability.

Yet, strategy alone isn't the sole benefactor of the MACD's revelations. It serves as an observational tool, a lens through which traders can assess the broader market sentiment. By analysing historical MACD patterns, traders can learn to anticipate shifts in momentum before they manifest in price changes. This anticipation enables proactive instead of reactive trading adjustments, aligning trades more closely with overarching market transformations.

The journey into understanding the MACD doesn't end here; it merely begins. With continuous practice and integration into your trading regimen, the MACD can transform from a mysterious acronym into an indispensable asset. Remember, while the MACD is powerful, it must be a part of a larger toolkit, complemented by rigorous risk management and thorough market analysis. Trading is both an art and a science, and the MACD bridges these realms, offering clarity amidst the crypto market's chaos.

Applying MACD to Crypto Trading

The Moving Average Convergence Divergence, or MACD, is often celebrated for its utility in traditional market analysis, but its application in the realm of crypto trading is nothing short of transformative. In an industry known for its volatility and rapid price movements, understanding how to wield the MACD effectively can be a game-changer. Let's unpack how you can integrate this powerful tool into your crypto trading arsenal with precision and confidence.

At its core, the MACD is a trend-following momentum indicator that reveals the relationship between two moving averages of a security's price. The two main components of the MACD indicator are the MACD line and the signal line. When the MACD line crosses above the signal line, it indicates potential bullish momentum, whereas a cross below the signal line suggests bearish momentum. This concept remains consistent whether you're examining equities, forex, or crypto assets. However, the magic truly lies in its adaptability to the elusive nature of crypto markets.

Crypto traders often rely on MACD to decipher not only the direction of a trend but also its strength. One practical application of MACD in crypto trading is identifying momentum shifts that precede substantial price movements. This is crucial, especially considering how quickly the value of cryptocurrencies can skyrocket or plummet. Critics might argue that lagging indicators like MACD may not keep pace with the swift tides of crypto, yet many traders have found success by adjusting the standard settings of the MACD to better fit their trading style and asset of choice.

Customising the MACD settings can help capture more timely signals suitable for cryptocurrencies. It's not uncommon to adjust the default 12, 26, and 9 settings to reflect shorter periods like 5, 35, and 5, especially in a market where seconds can make a difference. Shorter settings tend to offer more responsive signals, allowing traders to enter and exit positions more swiftly—an approach that can prove advantageous for day traders or those in highly volatile environments.

The histogram, a crucial part of the MACD, serves as an additional layer of insight. Representing the difference between the MACD line and the signal line, the histogram provides a visual cue of the momentum's intensity. A growing histogram suggests strengthening momentum, while a shrinking histogram could indicate fading momentum. For crypto traders, the histogram can function as a critical early-warning system, foretelling trend reversals or affirming current trajectories.

Some of MACD's most valuable insights emerge on timeframes of greater significance, such as daily and weekly charts. These timeframes filter out noise, allowing MACD to exhibit its prowess as a tool for assessing medium to long-term momentum. However, short-term intraday charts can also benefit from MACD when settings are adjusted to harness the everyday volatility of the crypto markets. Whether executing swift trades or holding positions over more extended periods, MACD's versatility continues to be an asset.

Moreover, combining MACD with other indicators can elevate your trading strategy to new heights. For instance, employing MACD alongside support and resistance levels or integrating it with volume analyses can offer a more comprehensive view. Such combinations help corroborate signals, reduce false positives, and bring more certainty to your trading decisions. It's this layered analysis approach that can refine entries and exits, ultimately leading to higher confidence and success rates in volatile market environments.

A common strategy employed by seasoned traders involves waiting for alignment between MACD crossovers and broader technical setups. For example, a bullish MACD crossover coinciding with a breakout above a resistance level often presents a high-probability trade. Such synchronisation confirms that the breakout is supported by increasing market momentum, thus mitigating some of the inherent risks associated with breakout trades.

While MACD is an indispensable tool, it’s not without its limitations. Given its foundation on historical data points, MACD doesn’t predict future price movements but analyses current trends. Consequently, applying MACD in isolation might lead to complacency, particularly in crypto's notoriously chaotic trading environments. As with any technical indicator, due diligence and a multifaceted approach are essential.

Risk management should never be overlooked when utilising MACD in your trading strategies. Setting proper stop-loss and take-profit points guided by the MACD’s signals can be crucial. This ensures that your risk exposure aligns with your trading goals and that potential losses remain manageable. A trade entered on an MACD bullish crossover might still encounter unexpected setbacks, highlighting the importance of having a holistic trading plan.

The journey to mastering MACD in crypto trading is as much about adaptability as it is about understanding the nuances of the markets. As you practice and gain experience, you'll better discern when and how to rely on MACD's guidance. Remember, every indicator in trading is just one piece of the puzzle. But when used skilfully, MACD has the power to illuminate paths through the intricate maze that is cryptocurrency trading.

Ultimately, the key to applying MACD to crypto trading lies in balancing its insights with a robust understanding of market dynamics, a well-thought-out trading plan, and emotional discipline. This trifecta will yield the confidence needed to make informed decisions, regardless of the turbulent crypto landscape. As you refine your trading techniques and embrace the patterns that unfold on the charts, you'll find that MACD is not merely an indicator but a trusted ally on your trading journey.

Chapter 12:
Advanced Indicator Combinations

Diving straight from our discussion on the powerful MACD in the previous chapter, we move towards a more intricate yet rewarding frontier: advanced indicator combinations. The core of this method lies in synthesising multiple technical indicators to unveil clearer trading signals, reducing false alarms and enhancing decision-making precision. Imagine the synergy of integrating RSI with MA crossovers or pairing Bollinger Bands with volume analyses to create a rich tapestry of insights. It's akin to having a conversation where each indicator plays a unique role, contributing its strengths to a more profound narrative. However, it's essential to remember that there's no one-size-fits-all approach; customising these combinations based on personal trading style and risk tolerance is key. By mastering these advanced strategies, you empower yourself, paving the way not just for informed trading but also for success in this dynamic crypto landscape.

Combining Indicators for Better Analysis

In the vast realm of crypto trading, harnessing the full potential of technical analysis requires more than just a basic understanding of individual indicators. Although each indicator can offer valuable insights on its own, the real magic happens when these tools are combined, creating a synergy that enhances your market insights. The process of combining indicators isn't just about randomly selecting them; it's about crafting a meaningful strategy that aligns with your trading goals and risk appetite.

At the core of combining indicators lies the idea of confirmation. By using multiple indicators, traders seek to validate signals, thereby reducing the noise that accompanies market movements. For instance, one might rely on the Moving Average Convergence Divergence (MACD) to detect momentum shifts and pair it with the Relative Strength Index (RSI) to gauge overbought or oversold conditions. This duo can provide a more comprehensive view, helping to make more informed trading decisions.

It's crucial to understand the strengths and limitations of each indicator you choose to combine. Some indicators, like moving averages, are great for identifying trends over various timeframes, whereas others, like the RSI, are more suited to pinpointing extreme market conditions. By selecting indicators with different roles, traders can cover multiple market perspectives: trend direction, momentum, and volatility, among others.

Equally important in the art of combining indicators is the avoidance of redundancy. Using multiple indicators that essentially provide the same information can lead to false confirmations and complicate decision-making processes. For instance, employing both the RSI and the Stochastic Oscillator may not be ideal, given their similar function of identifying overbought or oversold situations. Instead, pair them with a trend-following indicator like the MACD or a moving average to achieve a balanced view.

Trading strategies born from combining indicators can range from simple to complex. A relatively straightforward strategy might involve using a moving average crossover to confirm a trend and the RSI to gauge the entry or exit points, all while being set against the backdrop of key support and resistance levels. More advanced strategies might involve integrating volume indicators to add insight into the strength of a price move or utilizing candlestick patterns to further enhance entry and exit signals.

However, despite their power, it's important to remember that no combination of indicators can guarantee success. The crypto market's volatility is inherent, and unexpected news or events can override technical analysis. This is where customising strategies to personal comfort levels and backtesting them across different market conditions becomes critical. By understanding how your strategies perform historically, you can refine them to better manage risk and improve effectiveness.

Setting clear parameters for each indicator within your strategy can also help in maintaining consistency. For example, defining specific RSI levels for overbought and oversold conditions or setting fixed periods for moving averages can make your strategy more robust. Being adaptable, yet systematic, gives traders the flexibility to respond to market changes while maintaining discipline.

Of course, combining indicators effectively also requires an awareness of the broader market context. Understanding how macroeconomic factors, crypto-specific news events, and market sentiment influence price movements can enhance the reliability of your indicators. Incorporating elements of fundamental analysis will ensure your technical insights are grounded in market reality, providing a more holistic approach to trading.

The journey to mastering indicator combinations is one of experimentation and learning. Aspiring traders should start by exploring simple combinations and gradually increase complexity as understanding deepens. Engaging with trading communities and forums can also offer valuable insights and share experience-backed strategies that might inspire your path.

In conclusion, while individual indicators provide helpful snapshots of the market, their true value is unlocked when used in combination. Carefully crafting a strategy that combines these tools allows traders to reduce noise, confirm signals, and ultimately execute more informed trades. By following a process that includes diligent learning, thoughtful application, and constant adaptability, traders equip themselves not only to survive in the volatile world of crypto trading but to thrive within it.

Customising Indicator Strategies

When diving into the world of crypto trading, it's critical to appreciate the value and potential of customising indicator strategies. Each trader's journey is unique, which means that their strategies should be too. Tailoring strategies to fit individual needs and trading styles is akin to crafting a bespoke suit—precision, care, and understanding are essential. In any trading strategy, indicators serve as the compass, guiding decision-making by decoding market data into actionable insights. The art of customisation lies in skilfully blending various indicators to meet specific goals.

The first step in customising your strategy is understanding the purpose of each indicator you're considering. Indicators can generally be classified into lagging, leading, and real-time categories. Lagging indicators, such as moving averages, reflect past trends and can help identify the strength and continuation of these trends. Leading indicators, like the Relative Strength Index (RSI), attempt to predict future price movements and can indicate overbought or oversold conditions. Real-time indicators, often found in algorithms or certain momentum indicators, offer current market data that can prompt immediate trading actions.

Choosing the right combination of these indicators is crucial. To start, it's advisable to select a primary indicator that aligns with your core strategy—whether that be trend-following, momentum trading, or mean-reversion. For example, if you're focused on trend trading, the Moving Average Convergence Divergence (MACD) could serve as your foundation. From there, you can layer additional indicators that either confirm or complement the signals from your primary tool. This multi-faceted approach helps mitigate the risk of false signals and provides a more holistic view of the market.

While selecting indicators, keep in mind that more isn't always better. Overloading your charts with indicators can lead to analysis paralysis, where the sheer volume of information hinders decision-making. Instead, strive for balance. Select a handful of key indicators that align with your trading goals and practice discerning which signals truly warrant action. Being selective not only aids clarity but also sharpens your focus on the most pertinent aspects of market movement.

Next, it's crucial to adjust the settings of your chosen indicators to fit the unique characteristics of the crypto market and your personal trading rhythm. Crypto markets are notably volatile, and they trade around the clock, which can lead to rapid price fluctuations. Consequently, the default settings of many traditional indicators might not be optimal. Don't hesitate to experiment with timeframes or sensitivity settings. For example, while a standard RSI might use a 14-period setting, a shorter timeframe might be more suitable for a day trader seeking quick signals.

Moreover, integrating a backtesting phase into your strategy development is invaluable. Programs that allow you to test your customised indicator setups against historical data can reveal how your strategy might perform under various market conditions. Use this data to fine-tune your indicator settings and combinations. Remember, though, that past performance is not indicative of future results, so maintain flexibility and be prepared to adapt your strategies as the market evolves.

As you work on personalising your indicator strategies, don't forget the human element in trading. Committing to ongoing education and reflecting on your trades is as important as the indicators themselves. Many traders find success by keeping detailed trading journals, where they log their indicator settings, market conditions, and the thoughts behind each trade. Such practices not only aid in monitoring what works but also in identifying patterns in behaviour and performance that can lead to incrementally better trading practices.

It's equally critical to consider psychological resilience and emotional control when customising your strategies. Tailoring indicators can enhance decision-making, but they are only part of the story. A robust mental framework is essential for implementing these strategies consistently. Recognising when emotions are driving decisions can prevent reactive trading mistakes and improve your adherence to logically deduced strategies. Remember, the best-customised indicator strategies are those that align with your individual strengths, preferences, and psychological comfort zone.

Finally, engaging with a community or finding mentors can provide further insights into effective customisation techniques. Forums, webinars, and discussion groups can offer perspectives and tips that you might not have considered. Others' experiences can expand your understanding of how different indicator combinations work together, as well as alert you to potential pitfalls or innovative methods for interpretation. Collaboration and learning from others can significantly enhance your ability to craft a truly personalised strategy.

Incorporating custom strategies may seem daunting at first, but it's a rewarding process that sharpens your edge as a trader. By understanding each indicator’s role, streamlining your selection to prevent information overload, and continuously refining your approach, you set the stage for success. In the ever-shifting landscape of the crypto market, a well-crafted indicator strategy not only acts as a guide but also stands as a testament to your dedication, adaptability, and growth as a trader.

CHAPTER 13:

VOLUME ANALYSIS IN THE CRYPTO MARKET

In this chapter, we dive into the often underappreciated realm of volume analysis, an essential element for any aspiring crypto trader. Volume indicators serve as the market's voice, revealing the vigour behind price movements and helping traders discern genuine trends from deceptive waves. Understanding volume is like having a second sight; it offers a clearer view of market trends, confirming the strength or weakness of price actions. Engaging with volume analysis allows traders to spot accumulation and distribution phases, tipping off significant shifts before they manifest in price changes. As you hone your skill in analysing volume, you'll unlock deeper insights that can refine your trading strategies and edge closer to successful trades, transforming uncertainties into opportunities within the vibrant yet volatile crypto arena.

Importance of Volume Analysis

In the bustling world of the crypto market, understanding volume analysis could be your secret weapon for navigating the constant ebbs and flows. This facet of technical analysis, often overlooked by beginners, can provide invaluable insights into the market's pulse and a cryptocurrency's potential price movement. At its core, volume analysis is the examination of the amount of a particular asset being traded over a set period. It reflects the level of interest and commitment from traders and investors, essentially acting as the market's heartbeat. When rightly interpreted, volume can reveal trends before they manifest on price charts and empower you to make informed trading decisions.

Let's delve deeper into why volume holds such significance. Imagine you're analysing a crypto asset that's experiencing a sudden price rise. Without volume analysis, you might interpret this as a signal to buy. However, if this price movement occurs with low volume, it could be a false spike, potentially manipulated by a small number of traders. On the contrary, a price rise with high volume suggests genuine buyer interest, indicating a more reliable trend continuation. Thus, volume acts as a confirmation tool, lending weight to price movements.

Volume also plays a crucial role in identifying shifts in market momentum. When volume peaks drastically, it often signals an impending price reversal. This phenomenon occurs because as buying or selling intensifies, it reaches a saturation point, after which the market naturally retraces. For burgeoning crypto traders, spotting these shifts early can provide a strategic advantage, allowing you to anticipate and react to market changes before they fully materialise.

Another aspect where volume analysis proves indispensable is in understanding the concept of *liquidity*. High volume suggests ample liquidity which simply means there's a healthy number of buyers and sellers available to execute trades swiftly. For you as a trader, high liquidity means tighter spreads, less slippage, and better execution of orders. Conversely, low volume might indicate illiquidity, where price can move rapidly with little trade, increasing risk and the possibility of unpredictable or erratic market behaviours.

Beyond liquidity, volume analysis can also uncover trends much earlier than price charts alone. When used in tandem with other technical indicators such as moving averages or the Relative Strength Index (RSI), it can provide a clearer, more nuanced picture of market conditions. For instance, a moving average crossover might seem like a straightforward buy or sell signal. Still, without volume confirmation, its reliability could be questionable. By analysing the volume at these junctures, you can affirm the strength of such signals.

The world of crypto is rife with volatility and unpredictability. Consequently, volume analysis assumes another vital role: risk management. By helping to confirm market trends and reversals, it assists you in fine-tuning your entry and exit strategies, ultimately leading to better risk mitigation. Recognising when a trend is weakening or identifying potential market tops and bottoms can be the difference between maximising profits and incurring losses.

New entrants to the crypto market might find themselves overwhelmed by the vast array of data and indicators. However, focusing on volume analysis can simplify this complexity. By consistently observing volume in conjunction with price, you'll start to discern patterns and correlations unique to each cryptocurrency. This experience will hone your ability to react to market dynamics, bolstering your confidence in executing trades.

Another compelling reason to master volume analysis is its ability to debunk market noise. In the crypto world, it's not uncommon for sudden fads or fear-inducing news to create temporary disruptions in the market. Volume analysis helps you see beyond these transient anomalies, enabling you to establish whether a movement is supported by strong trader interest or is merely a blip. This clarity helps in maintaining a steady trading strategy and prevents knee-jerk reactions to every market whim.

Moreover, seasoned traders often use **volume spikes** as a harbinger of major market events. Sometimes, a sudden increase in volume, even while price remains relatively stable, suggests impending volatility. This prelude allows traders to prepare for potential opportunities or defend against swings, thus staying one step ahead of the curve. As such, incorporating volume analysis into your toolkit adds a layer of preparedness to navigate the unpredictable waters of crypto trading.

Finally, embracing volume analysis fosters a proactive trading mindset. Instead of solely reacting to price movements, you'll begin to anticipate them, positioning yourself more strategically in the market. This shift from a reactive to a proactive approach can dramatically enhance your trading effectiveness and improve your psychological resilience against market pressures.

In summary, the importance of volume analysis in the crypto market cannot be overstated. It serves as the bridge connecting technical insights with market psychology, offering a comprehensive view of genuine market activity and trader sentiment. By leveraging volume data, you can confirm trends, identify reversals, manage risks effectively, and even foresee significant market shifts. As you deepen your understanding and application of volume analysis, you'll find it becomes an indispensable facet of your trading strategy, guiding you towards more informed and successful trading decisions.

How to Leverage Volume for Trading

Volume analysis is one of the most valuable tools at a crypto trader's disposal. It's akin to listening to the market's pulse, providing insights far beyond mere price movements. Unlike price, which tells us what has happened, volume reveals the intensity behind those movements. It helps traders determine the strength of a trend or the weakness in a surge or plunge. For aspiring traders, mastering volume analysis can significantly enhance their trading strategies, leading to more informed and confident decision-making.

At its core, volume in trading refers to the number of tokens or contracts traded over a specific period. High volume indicates a significant level of interest and activity in a market, often coinciding with the confirmation or continuation of a trend. Conversely, low volume can hint at a potential reversal or stalling momentum. By examining volume, you can gain valuable insights into underlying market dynamics, complementing other technical analysis components.

Interpreting volume alongside price action is crucial. For instance, if a cryptocurrency's price rises on increasing volume, it's a positive sign that a strong and potentially sustainable trend is emerging. This scenario suggests genuine interest among traders and investors. On the other hand, if you observe a price increase on declining volume, it can indicate a lack of conviction among traders, possibly hinting at a looming reversal.

Volume can often precede price as well. Sometimes, unusual spikes in volume can serve as early warning signals for future price movements. While price might not immediately reflect these changes, volume surges may suggest an avalanche of pent-up interest or, conversely, disinterest waiting to express itself. Noting such volume spikes in conjunction with your other analysis methods can offer a strategic advantage.

One useful volume-related metric is the Volume-Weighted Average Price (VWAP). The VWAP provides a single price point in a day that takes account of trading volume, offering an average price weighted by volume. Traders utilise VWAP as a gauge of value for the time period assessed. If the current price is above the VWAP, it's perceived as relatively strong, while below it indicates potential weakness. Incorporating VWAP into your strategy can aid in identifying advantageous entry and exit points.

Another significant concept is volume divergence. This occurs when the volume trends in a direction opposite to the price. For instance, if a price is in an uptrend but volume is reducing, it suggests that fewer traders are participating in the rise, which might signal an impending reversal. Identifying and acting upon volume divergences can be a critical aspect of a savvy trader's toolkit, providing foresight before market movements swing.

Traders also employ volume profiles and range indicators. These tools analyse volume over specified price ranges, highlighting where the most trading activity occurs at certain levels. By understanding these points of substantial support and resistance, you can make more precise trading decisions and anticipate potential breakout levels.

To better comprehend volume dynamics, combining it with candlestick pattern recognition can be insightful. Candlestick patterns, especially in conjunction with volume data, can offer a rich tapestry of market sentiment. For instance, an engulfing pattern on high volume may signal a powerful trend reversal, while the same pattern on low volume might not carry the same weight.

Keep an eye out for volume spikes, which can be temporary or indicative of large institutional moves. These spikes often occur around significant news events or when the crypto asset breaks through a critical technical level. Being prepared to react when you spot these spikes is pivotal to capturing timely opportunities and avoiding potential traps.

Furthermore, recognising that different environments can change the interpretation of volume is vital. In a highly liquid market, volume signals may present differently compared to a less liquid one. Understanding these nuances enhances the robustness of your analysis, allowing for adjustments based on current market conditions.

As with all trading strategies, incorporating volume analysis requires practice and adaptability. It's not merely a magic bullet but rather a tool that complements your overall trading model. Continually refine your strategy, backtesting your approaches to understand what works well in various market conditions. By doing so, you amplify your confidence, readying yourself to face the ever-evolving crypto trading landscape.

Volume analysis isn't just about tracking numbers; it's about reading the market's energy and understanding trader sentiment. By applying it with precision and learning from each trade, you lay the groundwork for becoming a successful crypto trader. Know that every volume figure tells a story waiting to be discovered. As you grow more acquainted with these tales, you'll set the stage for developing strategies that resonate with the market's rhythm.

CHAPTER 14:

CHART PATTERNS FOR CRYPTO SUCCESS

Navigating the volatile world of cryptocurrency trading becomes significantly more manageable when you understand chart patterns. These visual formations are more than just random price movements; they're the language of the market, whispering potential future trends. Recognising common patterns like the head and shoulders, double tops and bottoms, and triangles is essential for crypto traders aspiring to achieve success. These patterns provide insights into possible continuations or reversals, allowing traders to anticipate the market's next move with confidence. By honing the skill to accurately interpret them, traders unlock the ability to position themselves strategically, riding on the momentum when it's favourable and retreating when caution is warranted. Mastery of chart patterns not only equips you with a technical edge but also fosters a disciplined and strategic trading mindset, crucial for thriving in the ever-evolving crypto landscape.

Common Crypto Chart Patterns

The world of crypto trading is a vibrant tapestry woven with patterns that reveal the underlying dynamics of the market. Chart patterns, an essential element of technical analysis, offer traders a visual representation of market sentiment and potential future price movements. Gaining a firm grasp of these patterns can be transformative for aspiring traders, empowering them with the ability to make informed decisions and increase their success rate.

Chart patterns can broadly be categorised into continuation and reversal patterns. Each category provides unique insights into the market's potential trajectory. Continuation patterns signal that the prevailing trend is likely to persist, while reversal patterns suggest that a trend change may be on the horizon. Understanding and identifying these patterns is crucial for crafting effective trading strategies.

Triangles are among the most common continuation patterns, frequently found in crypto charts. Triangles come in three varieties: ascending, descending, and symmetrical. Each type is defined by the direction in which it appears to 'point', indicating the likely breakout direction once the pattern is complete. Ascending triangles are bullish patterns, characterised by a series of higher lows and a level resistance line. They signal that buyers are gaining strength, often resulting in a breakout to the upside. On the other hand, *descending triangles*, with their lower highs and flat support line, are bearish patterns suggesting increased selling pressure. Symmetrical triangles, where the price converges in a series of lower highs and higher lows, can break out in either direction, making them a point of interest for traders monitoring volatility.

Head and Shoulders patterns are classic reversal patterns, signaling a potential trend change. The traditional head and shoulders pattern indicates a bearish reversal, typically occurring at the peak of an uptrend. It comprises three peaks – a higher middle peak (the head) flanked by two lower peaks (the shoulders). This pattern suggests that momentum is waning and a shift towards a downtrend might occur. Conversely, the inverse head and shoulders pattern, found at the trough of a downtrend, indicates a bullish reversal, signalling a potential shift to an upward trajectory.

The **double top and double bottom** formations are yet another pair of reversal patterns. A double top, resembling an 'M' shape on charts, suggests a bearish reversal. It forms when prices attempt to rise to a certain level twice but fail to sustain those highs, indicating resistance. Conversely, the double bottom pattern, resembling a 'W', is bullish. It forms at the end of a downtrend, indicating support and a potential upward reversal as buyers strengthen their position. Correctly identifying these patterns can provide traders with significant opportunities to enter and exit the market strategically.

Pennants, like triangles, are continuation patterns that occur after a strong price movement, known as the 'flagpole'. Following this, the price consolidates, forming a small symmetrical triangle or 'pennant' on the chart. Once the pattern completes, the price is expected to continue in the direction of the initial flagpole. Though often confused with triangles, pennants are typically shorter in duration and occur after a sharp price move.

Flags, akin to pennants, emerge following that strong price action. They form parallel lines, either slanting downwards during an uptrend or upwards during a downtrend. Their completion often signals the continuation of the dominant trend, making them valuable to traders looking to capture a second surge in price after consolidation.

Understanding these patterns involves more than just spotting shapes. It's about interpreting the battle between bulls and bears. Patterns like **cups and handles**, largely seen as bullish, illustrate this tug-of-war expertly. A cup and handle forms after a period of consolidation following an uptrend, where the price action resembles the shape of a cup. A breakout often follows, heralding an extension of the upward movement. Though akin to cups and handles, saucers represent longer-term consolidation and provide insights into prolonged market sentiment shifts.

An important consideration when analysing chart patterns is volume. A pattern gains credibility when supported by significant volume changes, as it confirms the strength behind the price movement. During breakouts, whether they be from a continuation or reversal pattern, an increase in volume often accompanies the shift, providing stronger validation.

Risk management and patience are vital components of any successful trading strategy. Chart patterns give an edge, but they aren't foolproof. Recognising pattern failures is equally as important as identifying successful formations. Not every pattern results in the expected price movement. Therefore, it's crucial to account for potential false signals and employ a disciplined approach to mitigate risks. Stop-loss orders and target settings based on these patterns can protect trades, preserving capital for future opportunities.

The dynamic nature of the crypto market can alter the conventional understanding and application of these patterns. Rapid innovation and volatility offer both challenges and opportunities. Therefore, traders must maintain flexibility in their strategies and adapt to evolving market conditions. Combining these classic patterns with indicators and other forms of analysis—while keeping an eye on the macroeconomic landscape—can provide a more comprehensive picture and hold the key to consistent success in the crypto space.

In conclusion, becoming proficient in recognising and interpreting common crypto chart patterns serves as a foundational skill for any trader seeking to navigate the often unpredictable waves of the cryptocurrency market. By integrating these patterns into a broader trading strategy, and continuously honing one's ability to interpret them in real time, traders are better positioned to seize opportunities and minimise risks. The art and science of pattern recognition are a continuous journey of learning and adapting, leading to greater control over trading outcomes.

Working with Continuation and Reversal Patterns

In the ever-evolving realm of crypto trading, understanding chart patterns can make the difference between success and missed opportunities. Recognising these patterns offers a glimpse into market sentiment and potential price directions, serving as a crucial tool for any serious trader. In this section, we'll dive into the world of continuation and reversal patterns, revealing how they can be used to their fullest potential to inform your trading decisions.

Chart patterns are visual representations on a price chart that suggest potential market movements based on historical data. Essentially, what has happened before often happens again, and there is profit to be made if you can spot these repetitions. While there are various patterns to consider in technical analysis, continuation and reversal patterns are among the most significant.

Continuation patterns, as the name suggests, indicate that the present trend in a market is likely to persist. They provide traders with a signal that consolidations or pauses in a trend are likely temporary and that the market will continue in the same direction. Some common continuation patterns include flags, pennants, and triangles. Each comes with unique characteristics and subtle nuances, requiring a keen eye and practice for accurate identification.

Flags are one of the simplest and most straightforward continuation patterns. Typically, a flag is identified by a brief counter-trend following a sharp price movement, often resembling a rectangle. The flagpole, which is the initial movement, tends to occur on strong volume, signalling robust market enthusiasm. Flags suggest the previous trend's resumption after the pause, enabling traders to set profitable entry and exit points.

Pennants resemble flags but take a more converging shape, forming small symmetrical triangles. They represent a short-term period of consolidation following a sharp price movement, and like flags, signal that the previous trend will continue once the pattern is complete. The key difference is that while flags move within parallel lines, pennants have converging trendlines.

Triangles, another continuation pattern, are classified into ascending, descending, and symmetrical triangles. Ascending triangles, often a bullish signal, form when there's a rising lower trendline amid a horizontal upper trendline. Falling trendlines in descending triangles point to bearish continuation signals. Symmetrical triangles indicate a period of indecision, which ultimately leads to a continuation of the previous trend—either bullish or bearish—once market participants decide the next direction.

In contrast, reversal patterns signal a change in the prevailing trend. These patterns indicate that the current trend is losing steam and that a turnaround is imminent. Identifying reversal patterns accurately can help traders exit positions before a significant market shift or enter a new trend early on. Classic examples of reversal patterns include head and shoulders, double tops and bottoms, and wedges.

The head and shoulders pattern is a popular reversal pattern. It's typically associated with market tops (head and shoulders) or market bottoms (inverse head and shoulders). This pattern consists of three peaks, where the centre peak is higher (for a head and shoulders top) or lower (for an inverse variant) than the two flanking shoulders. The completion of this pattern, confirmed by a 'neckline' break, often results in a directional shift in the market trend.

Double tops and bottoms are straightforward to identify and widely used by traders. A double top forms following an uptrend when the price peaks at a level twice and fails to breach that point. This indicates a potential bearish reversal. Conversely, a double bottom occurs during a downtrend, with the price hitting a low point twice, suggesting an incoming bullish reversal.

Wedges can act as both continuation and reversal patterns, though often regarded as more predictive of reversals. A rising wedge is a bearish pattern that signals a possible downturn, even when it appears during an uptrend. A falling wedge, contrariwise, is bullish and suggests a price upswing is possible after a period of consolidation.

Recognising these patterns is only part of the equation. Successful application involves confirming these patterns with other technical indicators and volume analysis. For instance, a breakout from a pattern backed by increased volume provides stronger confirmation. Without volume support, the breakout may be false, leading to potential trading pitfalls.

Developing an acute ability to accurately identify continuation and reversal patterns takes practice and persistence. Regularly reviewing historical charts and backtesting various scenarios enriches understanding and sharpens skills. It equips you to navigate the volatile crypto markets with greater ease and confidence.

Traders should combine their understanding of these patterns with sound risk management strategies. Setting appropriate stop-losses and targeting profits based on pattern projections helps mitigate potential losses. Furthermore, remaining flexible and adapting strategies as market conditions evolve ensures longevity and success in trading.

As you delve deeper into the lucrative world of crypto trading, the mastery of continuation and reversal patterns becomes an invaluable asset in your trading toolkit. They arm you with the foresight needed to stay ahead, anticipate market movements, and seize opportunities. Embrace this knowledge and incorporate it into your trading plan, setting the stage for a successful trading journey.

Chapter 15: Risk Management in Crypto Trading

In the dynamic world of crypto trading, effective risk management acts as a foundation for sustainable success. It doesn't just protect you from potential losses but empowers you to make informed decisions with confidence. Crafting a robust risk management strategy involves setting clear goals, determining your risk tolerance, and understanding the volatility intrinsic to cryptocurrency markets. Allocating only a portion of your capital to any single trade and employing stop-loss orders are methods seasoned traders use to mitigate adverse outcomes. Embrace the unpredictability of the market by continually adapting your strategy through both introspection and analysis of current trends. In doing so, you create a discipline that not only protects your investments but sharpens your instincts, ensuring longevity in the ever-evolving crypto landscape.

Creating a Risk Management Strategy

In the exhilarating world of crypto trading, crafting a robust risk management strategy is akin to building a solid foundation for success. Just as a sailor wouldn't venture into turbulent seas without navigational tools, traders must arm themselves with a comprehensive plan to weather the market's unpredictable tempests. At its core, a risk management strategy isn't merely an optional component of trading—it's an essential safeguard that can preserve your capital and sustain your market presence through the ebbs and flows of crypto volatility.

What's the first step in shaping this strategy? It's important to embrace the mindset that losses are a natural part of trading. Pretending the market will only go in your favour is a misstep that can lead to devastating consequences. Accepting that losses will occur allows traders to mitigate their psychological impact and approach trading with clarity and objectivity. To begin, set a clear limitation for the amount of capital you're willing to risk on any single trade. This is often called the *risk per trade*, and many seasoned traders suggest limiting this to a small percentage of your total trading capital—typically between 1% to 3%.

Determining the risk per trade involves not only setting a percentage limit but also understanding your risk tolerance and investment goals. Have you defined how much discomfort you're willing to tolerate when a trade turns against you? While some traders can stomach higher risks for potentially higher rewards, others might prioritise a steady, controlled growth of their portfolio. Tailoring your risk per trade percentage based on these personal factors ensures that your strategy remains aligned with your financial aspirations and emotional capacity.

Once you've set your risk threshold, it's time to delve into position sizing. The size of your trade directly correlates with your risk per trade. By balancing the two, you can consistently apply your risk management principles across different market conditions. It's not uncommon for traders to employ a simple formula: dividing the dollar amount they're willing to lose by the distance between their trade entry and stop-loss point. This calculation provides the trade size, ensuring the loss won't exceed predefined limits, no matter how the market moves. Such rigour in decision-making forms the backbone of a disciplined trading routine.

Stop-loss orders are invaluable tools in this equation. They act as pre-set failure points, triggering automatic exits from losing trades to prevent further losses. The strategic placement of stop-loss orders should account for market volatility and the specific characteristics of the traded cryptocurrency. By setting stop-loss levels that respect both personal risk tolerance and market noise, traders can protect their capital from dramatic price swings while avoiding unnecessary exits on minor fluctuations.

Beyond stop-losses, the concept of position correlation profoundly influences risk management. In forex or equity markets, correlations come from trading pairs or baselines; in crypto, the shifting sentiment towards major cryptocurrencies can ripple through the market. If all your positions are heavily tied to Bitcoin's performance, for example, a downturn could disproportionately affect your portfolio. Diversifying across cryptocurrencies with different use cases and market influences can buffer against such systemic risks while also leveraging various opportunities.

Effective risk management also requires a keen awareness of market liquidity. Illiquid assets can present challenges when trying to execute trades, leading to slippage—where trades happen at a different price than expected. Managing slippage risk is a nuanced dance of matching trade size with asset liquidity and adjusting entry and exit plans to minimise impacts. High liquidity typically means greater flexibility in executing trades without significant price movement, a key consideration when planning your strategy.

Moreover, a successful risk management strategy anticipates the broader market environment. Familiarise yourself with macroeconomic factors and developments that could influence the cryptocurrency landscape, such as regulatory changes or technological breakthroughs. Staying informed allows for proactive adjustments to your strategy, aligning with new trends or avoiding pitfalls before they become debilitating risks. Knowledge is indeed power in the fast-paced crypto world.

While we've delved into the technical aspects of risk management, the mental framework accompanying them is equally vital. Cultivating discipline involves maintaining adherence to your rules, devoid of emotional interference. The temptation to deviate is ever-present, especially in volatile conditions, but steadfast commitment distinguishes thriving traders from those constantly chasing losses. Developing self-awareness and control over emotional responses fortifies your strategy, allowing you to act with rationality and patience.

Finally, risk management isn't a one-time effort. It's a dynamic process of continuous evaluation and improvement. Regularly review your trading results and identify any deviations or areas for refinement. Reflect on past trades, both successful and unsuccessful, to extract lessons that could enhance future performance. By iteratively developing your strategy, you're sculpting a progressively resilient approach capable of thriving in the evolving crypto markets.

Creating a risk management strategy goes beyond shielding yourself from potential downturns—it's about empowering yourself as a trader. With a well-constructed plan, you gain the confidence to venture into the market with a clear understanding of the potential risks and rewards. In doing so, you harness the tools and knowledge necessary to achieve sustainable success in the capricious world of crypto trading.

Tools for Minimising Trading Risks

Managing risks effectively in the highly volatile realm of crypto trading isn't just an option; it's a necessity. With prices swiftly changing direction, traders must arm themselves with the right tools to safeguard their investments. Amongst the arsenal of risk minimisation tools, there are several indispensable mechanisms every trader should explore.

First and foremost, **stop-loss orders** and **take-profit orders** are powerful when used correctly. These are automatic instructions set to buy or sell once a cryptocurrency reaches a predetermined price, preventing potential losses from being realised beyond an acceptable level. By configuring these orders based on one's risk appetite, traders are not only safeguarding their capital but also removing emotional decision-making from the equation. Additionally, setting these orders ensures a disciplined approach, enabling traders to secure profits without succumbing to greed.

Adopting a well-defined **position sizing strategy** is another pivotal approach to managing risk. Imagine diving into trades arbitrarily, allocating different sums each time; the inconsistency can lead to disproportionate losses. Position sizing helps traders determine how much they should invest in a particular trade based on their account size and risk tolerance, ensuring they don't overcommit to single trades. By using a percentage of their total capital, traders can effectively withstand a series of losing trades without catastrophic results.

Another indispensable tool in the crypto trader's toolkit is **diversification**. While putting all one's eggs in a single basket might yield significant returns, it's equally likely to result in substantial losses during adverse market movements. By diversifying across different cryptocurrencies and sectors within the crypto market, traders can mitigate specific risks associated with any one particular asset. Diversification helps stabilise the overall volatility of a portfolio, providing a buffer against sharp declines from individual assets.

Utilising leverage prudently might sound attractive for those looking to amplify their returns, but it comes with heightened risks. Leveraged trading allows traders to control a larger position with a relatively small amount of capital. If things go as intended, the rewards can be remarkable. However, it's vital to remember that leverage doesn't discriminate—it magnifies losses just as it does gains. Therefore, understanding the inherent risks and setting strict limits on leverage utilisation is crucial.

Volatility analysis serves a critical role in risk management by helping traders understand market instability. By gauging the price fluctuations of cryptocurrencies over a specific period, traders can anticipate potential shifts and better prepare for sudden changes. Tools that track and analyse volatility enable traders to adapt their strategies to varying market conditions, thereby reducing unexpected surprises. These assessments are often supplemented by historical data to provide a broader context, allowing traders to perceive patterns and prepare accordingly.

Furthermore, **hedging** acts as a risk management strategy that allows traders to protect an investment by taking an offsetting position in a related security. In the world of crypto, this could mean holding a mix of cryptocurrencies—some perceived as 'safe assets' during market turmoil or employing instruments like options that act as a safety net. Although hedging comes with added costs, when exercised thoughtfully, it provides a layer of protection against adverse market movements.

Technical analysis tools like moving averages, RSI (Relative Strength Index), and MACD (Moving Average Convergence Divergence) also play a significant role in assessing trading risks. By providing insights into market trends and momentum, these indicators help traders make more informed decisions. For instance, recognising when a currency is overbought or oversold assists in timing trades better, minimising risks associated with poor entry or exit points.

Importantly, **continuous learning** and **adapting** to new market trends cannot be overstated. The crypto landscape is dynamic; new technologies, regulations, and macroeconomic factors continuously influence it. Traders who remain volatile to these changes and educate themselves on emerging trends and tools inevitably preserve a competitive edge. Attending webinars, reading market analyses, and engaging with seasoned traders can enhance one's understanding and decision-making capabilities.

Regularly **reviewing and updating your trading plan** is integral to managing risks effectively. As market conditions and personal circumstances evolve, the initial assumptions and strategies underpinning your trading plan might become obsolete. An adaptable trading plan, one which considers past performance and adjusts for future contingencies, keeps a trader grounded amidst fluctuating landscapes.

Lastly, one must never overlook the significance of managing one's *emotions*. Emotional trading often leads to impulsive decisions that deviate from sound analysis and strategy adherence. Employing techniques to detach emotions from trades, whether it's through automation of some processes or practising mindfulness, ensures decisions are rooted in logic rather than fear or greed. Balance and clarity in mindset can play just as critical a role in risk management as any technical tool.

To sum up, while crypto trading inevitably involves risk, with the right suite of tools and strategies, the apparent chaos can be navigated effectively. Risks can't be entirely eliminated, but they can be controlled and, to a significant extent, predetermined. By leveraging stop-losses, disciplined position sizing, and embracing continuous learning, traders are well-positioned not only to protect their capital but to thrive in a competitive market. True success in crypto trading comes not just from bold actions but from meticulous planning and risk management.

Chapter 16:

Trading Psychology: Mastering Your Mind

To succeed in the unpredictable waters of crypto trading, it's crucial to cultivate the art of mastering your mind. Every trader knows that strategies and technical skills are only part of the equation; the true challenge often lies within. Fear and greed can cloud judgement, driving impulsive decisions that stray from well-laid plans. Recognising the psychological barriers that emerge during trading and learning to overcome them can be the decisive factor separating profitable trades from emotional hastiness. To navigate these mental fluctuations, develop strong self-discipline by setting clear goals and sticking to them, even when market tides turn unexpectedly. The power of reflection and being aware of your own emotional triggers cannot be overstated. By incorporating regular self-analysis and mindfulness, you create a mental framework that remains resilient against the whirlwind of the crypto market. Remember, in the world of trading, mastering your mind doesn't just safeguard your investments—it forges a path to consistently rational, and potentially more lucrative, trading decisions.

Understanding Trading Psychology

Diving into the realm of trading psychology is not just about knowing what emotions traders experience but understanding why they have such a profound impact on decision-making. The world of crypto trading is exhilarating yet daunting. It can thrust you into a rollercoaster of emotions—euphoria from a rising market, despair during a crash, and the anxiety of uncertainty. For many, the battle isn't just against market forces, but against inner turmoil.

Recognising the role that fear and greed play is crucial. These two emotions, often described as the most impactful in trading, can skew judgment and cloud reasoning. Fear can halt you from entering a promising market position, while greed can keep you holding onto a position far longer than prudent. Experienced traders learn that controlling these emotions is vital to maintaining a balanced strategy.

Every trader, at some point, confronts the challenge of emotional overreach. It's common to hear stories about how a single emotional choice led to significant financial loss. So why do traders allow emotion to interfere, even when they're aware of the risks? The answer lies partly in how humans are wired. Our brains are naturally risk-averse and often react to short-term stimuli rather than long-term evaluations. Consequently, learning to override these instinctual responses is part of mastering trading psychology.

Discipline and patience are traits often cited by trading veterans as essential tools. When you couple discipline with a well-researched trading plan, you can steer clear of emotional pitfalls. Traders who adhere to their predefined strategies tend to make more coherent decisions. It's about training your mind to stick to the plan, even when your emotions are begging you to do otherwise.

Perspective plays a significant role. Viewing losses as learning opportunities rather than significant setbacks can shift your entire trading experience. Losses are inevitable in trading, but they don't define you. Their purpose is to inform and improve your future strategies. Every misstep should be assessed calmly, allowing you to refine your approach and evolve.

Visualisation and mental preparation can also be valuable tools for managing emotions. Before opening the trading app, take a moment to envisage various scenarios, including those unfavourable outcomes. By mentally preparing for losses and gains, you can reduce the surprise element and foster a more balanced emotional response.

Some traders find meditation and mindfulness exercises beneficial for maintaining emotional equilibrium. Practices such as these can centre your thoughts and foster a calm mind—crucial for making rational trading decisions. Over time, incorporating such practices can substantially reduce the instances of knee-jerk reactions to market fluctuations.

Building a supportive environment is another cornerstone of effective trading psychology. Whether through online communities, forums, or relationships with fellow traders, discussing successes and failures can provide a grounded view of your trading journey. Others can often see what you might overlook and offer insights into different approaches you might not have considered.

It's important to recognise that trading psychology doesn't just impact emotional highs or lows. It influences every small decision, each choice of entry or exit point, and every adjustment to your trading strategy. Enhancing trading psychology isn't about attaining an emotionless state; rather, it's about striking a harmony between emotion and logic.

An understanding of your strengths and weaknesses forms an integral part of mastering your mind. Trading isn't a one-size-fits-all scenario. Lean into your personal style and preferences. Are you more suited to quick decisions, or do you resonate with longer, methodical approaches? By aligning your strategy with your personality, you weave a safety net that supports and strengthens your psychological resilience.

Regular self-reflection is a practice worth embracing. Journaling your trades, noting your emotions at each step, and analysing these after the fact can illuminate recurrent patterns in your decision-making processes. Over time, this activity sheds light on psychological triggers that might otherwise remain unnoticed. Awareness of these can serve as the first step toward adjusting and improving.

Ultimately, mastering trading psychology is a journey. One that requires continuous dedication and adaptation. As you navigate through the volatile tides of the crypto markets, remember, the most successful traders are not those without emotions but those who have learned to integrate them into a robust trading framework.

Crafting a mental edge takes time, effort, and often a shift in mindset. Yet, the rewards—a clearer assessment of risk, a balanced emotional state, and a higher likelihood of sustaining success—are invaluable. In understanding trading psychology, you not only master the market's nuances but also achieve profound personal growth.

Overcoming Emotional Barriers

In the vibrant and often volatile world of crypto trading, mastering the psychological aspects of trading is as crucial as understanding market analysis. The art of chart interpretation and technical analysis needs to be complemented with a robust mental framework. Enter the challenge of overcoming emotional barriers. For many aspiring traders, emotions like fear, greed, and impatience create hurdles just as formidable as the complexities of the market itself.

Imagine standing at the edge of a cliff, hesitant to leap. This is akin to the fear faced by traders when contemplating a trade. Fear, although inherently protective, can inhibit a trader's ability to make rational decisions. Suddenly, past losses haunt their minds and magnify uncertainties, leading to hesitation or even avoidance. Awareness is the first step. Recognising that fear is a natural response rather than a personal flaw can help traders confront it. Armed with this understanding, they can begin to rationalise their emotions, reminding themselves of their research and strategy before allowing fear to dictate their actions.

There's an adrenaline rush associated with seeing a favourable price movement. It's tempting to latch onto that excitement and let greed take the reins, pushing a trader to jump into transactions without a second thought. However, just as fear can be paralysing, unchecked greed can lead to impulsive decisions and excessive risk-taking. Aspiring traders may find themselves buying at peaks or doubling down on risky trades, often leading to regret. Key to managing this is establishing predefined goals and sticking to them. Emphasise the importance of discipline over short-lived euphoria inherent in impulsive trading.

Wake up to impatience as another subtle saboteur. In crypto trading, impatience can drive traders to take ill-conceived actions, often abandoning well-laid plans for hastier, riskier alternatives. The immediate gratification of a successful trade is seductive, but the allure comes at a cost if strategic patience isn't practised. Acknowledge the value of waiting for the right opportunities and sticking to them. It's crucial to reinforce patience by setting realistic expectations and focusing on long-term success rather than short-term gains.

Developing emotional resilience isn't about suppressing emotions. Rather, it involves recognising them, understanding their impact, and learning to navigate them effectively. Meditation and mindfulness can be powerful tools in this journey. Such practices encourage a calm, reflective mindset, helping traders maintain clarity and perspective. A few minutes of meditation at the start of your trading session can set the tone for a controlled approach, although any technique that works can be applied consistently.

Consider emotional safety nets, like setting alerts and reminders, to step back and reassess decisions during high-stakes situations.

Building a robust support network also plays a vital role in overcoming emotional barriers. Engaging with other traders and mentors allows for shared experiences and communal learning. Conversations can offer insights into how emotions influence behaviour and provide strategies to handle common emotional pitfalls. By interacting with seasoned traders, markets seem less intimidating, and peers provide the encouragement needed to persist through challenging periods.

Practising self-reflection is another transformative tool. Regularly analysing trades with an objective eye can uncover patterns in emotional responses. Did a recent loss trigger a fear of re-entering the market? Was a lucrative trade driven more by luck than strategy, thereby feeding greed? By documenting and reviewing these episodes in a trading journal, traders can identify triggers and devise specific approaches to counteract them. This process also breeds humility, a trait that is indispensable in an ever-evolving market landscape.

It's essential to also consider the environment in which trading occurs. Physical surroundings can impact mental states—clutter and chaos are distractions that foster anxiety. Creating a serene, organised space dedicated to trading can enhance focus and reduce stress. Equally, establishing a routine that includes breaks can prevent burnout. Step away from the screen periodically to recharge, as persistence is a marathon, not a sprint.

Acknowledge that setbacks are inevitable in crypto trading, as they are in any form of investment. They're part of the learning curve, not the end of the trading journey. Reframing these experiences as opportunities for growth can alleviate the sting of failure. Adopt a mindset that champions learning—every incorrect decision teaches lessons that no textbook ever could. Make peace with mistakes, reconstructing them into stepping stones on the road to mastery.

Ultimately, the key to overcoming emotional barriers lies within the balance between confident action and cautious introspection, a balance between the strategic mind and the emotional heart. Success stems from a foundation built on education, planning, and adaptability. The battle against emotional volatility is not won overnight; it is a continual effort, reflective of both personal and professional growth. In conquering these barriers, aspiring traders don't just dominate the charts, but also themselves.

Chapter 17: Backtesting Your Crypto Strategies

As you journey deeper into the art and science of crypto trading, the necessity of backtesting becomes ever more apparent. It is the process that arms you with historical performance insights, setting the stage for what might lie ahead. By meticulously evaluating past data and scrutinising old trades against your current strategies, you can unearth patterns and tweak approaches that improve potential success. Imagine having the foresight to understand how your strategies would have performed without risking any capital; it's not just advantageous—it's essential. A good backtest isn't just about numbers; it involves the critical analysis of how well a strategy aligns with real-world behaviours and market conditions, honing your intuition. Ultimately, effective backtesting empowers traders to refine their strategies, making adjustments based on historical outcomes, and offers a glimpse into how they might navigate future market waves with confidence and precision. As you delve into the world of backtesting, remember that this tool can transform you from a hopeful trader into a strategic thinker, capable of leveraging the past to illuminate your path forward in the exhilarating world of crypto trading.

Importance of Backtesting

In the dynamic and fast-paced world of crypto trading, the significance of backtesting cannot be overstated. It serves as the foundational block upon which successful trading strategies are built. By simulating past trading conditions, traders can assess how well their strategies would have performed in real-market scenarios. This is not a mere exercise in theory; it provides tangible insights that can differentiate between trading success and failure.

An essential aspect of backtesting is its ability to remove speculative guesswork from the equation. Traders often fall into the trap of relying on intuition or emotion-driven decisions, especially in a market as volatile as crypto. Backtesting brings objectivity to the table by allowing traders to analyse historical data against predefined strategies. Through this process, traders can clearly see patterns, strengths, and weaknesses within their strategies, offering crucial lessons for future trading.

Imagine entering a market without any knowledge of how your strategy might fare. It’s akin to embarking on a journey with an untested map. Sure, you might reach your destination by chance, but more often than not, you'll find yourself lost and frustrated. Backtesting equips you with a reliable map, grounded in factual data and evidence. This enables traders to traverse the crypto landscape confidently, minimising risks that come from operating in the dark.

Furthermore, backtesting empowers traders to refine their strategies. Once a strategy has been tested against historical data, traders can identify the areas that need improvement. It offers a clear feedback loop, illustrating what works and what doesn’t under specific market conditions. Adjustments can then be made to optimise performance, thereby enhancing one's trading arsenal. This iterative refinement is indispensable for staying adaptive and responsive to the ever-evolving crypto markets.

Confidence in trading decisions is another significant by-product of backtesting. When traders are aware of how their strategies have performed historically, they develop a deeper sense of conviction in their trades. This confidence is vital, especially when the market behaves unpredictably, enabling traders to hold steadfast in their positions rather than reacting impulsively. With backtested data at their disposal, traders are equipped to make informed decisions that are not swayed by the emotional highs and lows of the market.

Beyond its practical benefits, backtesting introduces a psychological edge by enhancing trading discipline. When traders see the correlation between discipline in applying their backtested strategies and positive outcomes, it instils a level of discipline necessary for sustained success. By reinforcing the importance of sticking to a well-tested plan, backtesting becomes a cornerstone of responsible trading behaviour.

However, it is imperative to acknowledge the limitations of backtesting. While it provides valuable insights based on past data, it cannot predict future market movements with absolute certainty. The crypto market is notoriously unpredictable, influenced by myriad factors ranging from technological advancements to regulatory changes. Nonetheless, backtesting enables a trader to be as prepared as possible for future market conditions by learning from historical precedent.

Moreover, the effectiveness of backtesting hinges on the quality and relevance of historical data. Traders must ensure they have access to comprehensive and accurate datasets that truly reflect past market conditions. Skewed or incomplete data can lead to misleading conclusions, which in turn can undermine the effectiveness of subsequent trading strategies. Therefore, selective data integrity and thoroughness are paramount.

Despite these challenges, backtesting remains an indispensable tool in a trader's toolkit. It provides the empirical evidence needed to validate or invalidate trading hypotheses, transforming speculative approaches into structured strategies. The lessons drawn from backtesting shape and mould traders into more analytical and strategic decision-makers, which is a vital attribute in the world of crypto trading.

The journey towards mastering crypto trading starts with understanding the power of informed strategies. Backtesting is the incubator for such strategies, laying a firm foundation on which traders can build robust and resilient strategies. Through diligent backtesting, aspiring traders can navigate the tumultuous waters of crypto markets with clarity and confidence, continuously evolving through lessons drawn from the past.

How to Backtest Effectively

Backtesting is a vital component of crafting successful crypto trading strategies. It offers a structured way to evaluate how a trading strategy might have performed in the past, providing insights that might help prevent costly errors in real-time trading. To backtest effectively, it's crucial to not only understand the mechanics of this process but also to develop a mindset aligned with thorough analysis and critical thinking. Let's delve into how to execute backtesting robustly and yield insights that power your trading endeavours.

Firstly, defining clear objectives is indispensable. Understand what you aim to achieve through backtesting. Whether you're assessing the profitability of a particular strategy, testing risk management techniques, or simply becoming familiar with market dynamics, having a pre-determined goal will guide your process. Goals provide the lens through which you'll analyse data and draw conclusions, ultimately refining your approach to fit specific trading environments or personal risk appetite.

Choose your data wisely. Historical data quality is the bedrock of effective backtesting. Ensure the data set spans a sufficiently long period to cover various market cycles, as different conditions can profoundly impact strategy performance. High-frequency data might offer more granular insights, particularly if you're developing strategies for day trading. In contrast, longer time frames might suffice for strategies aiming to capture broader market trends. Whichever route you take, ensure the data source is reliable to avoid skewed results.

Next, replicate realistic trading conditions. Backtesting should mimic the environment in which you'll execute trades, incorporating factors such as transaction costs, slippage, and spread variations. These elements, often overlooked, can drastically alter a strategy's performance and perceived profitability if absent from the analysis. Incorporate them into your model from the start to ensure results reflect real-world viability and address potential challenges head-on.

The choice of backtesting software can significantly affect your analysis' depth and accuracy. Various tools are available, from simple spreadsheets to dedicated backtesting platforms equipped with advanced features like algorithmic strategy testing and optimisations. Select one that matches your technical proficiency and the complexity of the strategies you're testing. While sophisticated software can handle complex models, ensure you grasp its functions entirely to make informed adjustments and interpretations.

Document your process rigorously. Detailed documentation not only aids in replicating results but also enhances the learning process. Record every parameter, hypothesis, and anomaly encountered. This comprehensive record serves as a reference for future strategy modifications and as a foundation for developing new strategies. Additionally, should you require external feedback or wish to share insights, such a document provides all necessary information in a digestible format.

Monitor for overfitting, a common pitfall in backtesting. Overfitting occurs when your strategy becomes too tailored to historical data, capturing noise rather than genuine market signals. A tell-tale sign of overfitting is consistently high profitability in backtests but poor performance when applied live. To mitigate overfitting, adopt robust out-of-sample testing techniques and validate your strategy across different time frames and market conditions. Simplicity often enhances robustness; complex strategies with numerous parameters are more prone to overfitting.

Utilise a walk-forward analysis as part of your testing methodology. This approach divides your dataset into multiple segments, applying your strategy iteratively across these periods to determine adaptability and scalability. By testing strategies incrementally over time, this technique helps gauge how well a strategy might adapt to shifting market dynamics. The iterative nature of walk-forward analysis closely mirrors the sequential decisions traders must make in real-world scenarios, providing an added layer of realism to your backtesting results.

Once you've backtested a strategy, critically evaluate your outcomes. While positive results may seem promising, it's essential to remain sceptical and assess whether the strategy genuinely exploits a market inefficiency or merely capitalises on a specific dataset's peculiarities. Consider benchmarking results against established indices or alternative strategies to provide context on their relative success. Additionally, seek to understand strategy behaviours during different market conditions to ensure they align with your risk management principles.

Backtesting should be an iterative process. It's unlikely that a strategy will emerge optimally from a single round of testing. Be prepared to refine and adapt, re-evaluating key hypotheses and assumptions in light of new data. This iterative approach not only hones your strategies but also deepens your understanding of market behaviours and your trading philosophy.

Finally, remain flexible and open to feedback. Engaging with a community of traders or consulting experts can provide valuable perspectives and highlight potential blind spots. These interactions enhance your strategies and can introduce new methods or ideas you might not have considered. Keep your conclusions under constant review, and remain open to recalibrating strategies in response to new information or changing trends in the crypto markets.

In mastering the art of backtesting, you're not just optimizing trading strategies; you're building a framework of critical evaluation and continuous learning. This foundation empowers you to navigate the unpredictable waters of crypto trading with confidence and clarity. Embrace this journey of discovery, knowing that each test brings you one step closer to informed, successful trading. Continuously refine your approach, let data guide your decisions, and stay nimble in an ever-evolving market landscape.

CHAPTER 18:

DEVELOPING YOUR CRYPTO TRADING PLAN

Embarking on the journey of creating a robust crypto trading plan is a pivotal step towards achieving consistent success in the volatile world of cryptocurrency. At the core of an effective plan lies a clear strategy that aligns with your personal risk tolerance and trading style, considering both short-term aspirations and long-term goals. Start by defining your objectives, as clarity here will guide your subsequent actions. Incorporate comprehensive research and analysis techniques you've mastered, weaving together elements of fundamental and technical analysis. Your plan should encompass specific entry and exit criteria, ensuring emotional detachment in the heat of market movements. Decide on the capital allocation for each trade to maintain financial discipline, making adjustments as you refine your understanding of market dynamics. Furthermore, rigorously implement risk management strategies to protect your capital during periods of market turbulence. By tailoring your plan, understanding your strengths, and learning from every trade, you create a personalised roadmap that not only mitigates risks but also captures opportunities in this rapidly evolving market landscape. Remember, a well-developed trading plan isn't just a set of rules; it's an evolving framework that adapts with your growth as a trader.

Components of a Crypto Trading Plan

Embarking on the crypto trading journey without a concrete plan is like setting sail without a map. It's essential to know not just where you want to go, but how you're going to get there. The components of a crypto trading plan are akin to the tools and guidelines you'd require to navigate the unpredictable waters of the crypto market. By integrating these elements, you'll better understand your trading approach, mitigate risks, and optimise your chances of success.

A pivotal part of any trading plan is setting clear *trading objectives*. What are you seeking to achieve with your trading? Defining these objectives is crucial. Some traders might aim for a steady income, while others are in for short-term gains. Your trading goals should be specific, measurable, achievable, relevant, and time-bound (SMART). By formulating these goals, you can tailor your strategies and monitor your progress. The journey of trading becomes not just about the destination but the milestones you achieve along the way.

The next component to consider is your *risk tolerance*. Every trader has a different appetite for risk, and understanding yours is fundamental to shaping your trading plan. Are you able to withstand the volatile swings often associated with crypto assets? Determining your risk tolerance will guide you in selecting appropriate assets and help you decide how much capital to invest in each trade. It's a safeguard, ensuring you don't bite off more than you can chew when market movements are not in your favour.

Linked closely with risk tolerance is your *capital allocation strategy*. Knowing how to effectively allocate your resources can impact your returns significantly. This involves deciding how much to invest in any single trade or asset and ensuring diversification to spread risk. Use well-defined principles to distribute your capital in a way that maximises potential returns while keeping losses manageable. An efficient allocation strategy will reflect your goals and risk profile, paving the way for disciplined and structured trading.

No trading plan is complete without a robust *risk management strategy*. While diving into the depths of risk management, it's essential to define rules for when to exit a trade, either to cut losses or to protect profits. Consider stop-loss and take-profit levels that align with your trading objectives and strategies. Implementing such safeguards is not just about preserving capital; it's about optimising your trading efforts so that you can grow sustainably over time. This disciplined approach to risk is crucial in a market as speculative and tumultuous as crypto.

Another crucial component is the constant evaluation of *market conditions and analysis*. No market remains static, particularly the crypto market, which is known for its rapid shifts. Regularly analysing market trends and reviewing chart patterns keeps you informed and adaptable. This analysis will inform your trading decisions and refine your strategic approach. Let the charts and data guide your actions, not emotions or unverified news sources. A methodical approach to analysis positions you to react skilfully to market shifts, a hallmark of seasoned traders.

In any effective trading plan, there's a need for a *trading journal* to track progress and enhance learning. Documenting each trade provides valuable insights into your performance. Note down the strategy applied, the asset traded, entry and exit points, and the rationale behind decisions. By revisiting your trades, both winners and losers, you glean insights into patterns of success and areas requiring improvement. A trading journal is your mirror, reflecting your trading psyche and helping you evolve by avoiding past mistakes and capitalising on winning strategies.

Let's not overlook the importance of *time management* as an integral part of your plan. Recognise the time commitment required for active trading, and set aside dedicated periods for both market analysis and actual trading. Whether you're trading part-time or as a full-time endeavour, structuring your day around crypto activities ensures that you remain focused and are less likely to miss opportunities or make impulsive decisions. Good time management brings consistency to your trading, transforming actions into habitual practices that benefit your overall strategy.

Embrace the flexibility offered by a *strategy evaluation and adaptation process*. Any trading strategy requires periodic assessment and recalibration based on performance and market evolution. Stay open to learning from market developments and adapting strategies as necessary. The crypto landscape is dynamic, and what works today might not be the case tomorrow. Keeping your strategy fluid yet grounded in sound principles ensures you remain a step ahead, turning challenges into opportunities for growth.

Lastly, a strong *psychological framework* can't be downplayed when developing your trading plan. Trading isn't just a test of skill but a test of mental fortitude. Be prepared to face setbacks and work on maintaining a balanced emotional perspective. Understand your own behavioural biases and establish a framework for controlling emotional responses like fear or greed. By cultivating a disciplined mindset, you inherently strengthen your trading plan, ensuring decisions are made out of logic instead of impulsive emotional reactions.

Crafting an effective crypto trading plan is like designing a guiding compass. Each element complements the other, forging a comprehensive approach to navigating unpredictable markets. From defining your goals to instituting rigorous risk management methods, the components of a well-rounded trading plan provide the structure and discipline necessary for mastering the art of crypto trading. Engage with these components earnestly, and you'll find yourself not merely participating in the crypto market but mastering it.

Customising Your Plan for Success

Creating a tailored crypto trading plan is like developing a unique blueprint for your financial journey. While standard strategies exist, personalising your approach is crucial. This means considering your financial goals, risk tolerance, and trading experience. Think of your plan as a living document; it's not set in stone but something that evolves with your growing insights and expertise in the crypto market.

One of the first steps in customising your plan is to clearly articulate your goals. Are you aiming for steady growth over time or rapid gains through more aggressive trades? Each objective comes with its own set of strategies and risk management techniques. It's important to be realistic here, setting achievable targets that can keep you motivated and focused.

Understanding your risk tolerance is another critical factor. How much are you willing to lose on a trade without it affecting your overall financial stability? This can be tied to your emotional resilience as a trader. If the stress of volatile swings keeps you awake at night, a more conservative approach might be best. On the other hand, some traders thrive in dynamic environments and may choose to embrace more daring strategies.

Customisation also involves aligning your trading plan with your lifestyle. Consider how much time you can dedicate to trading. If you have a full-time job or familial obligations, you might opt for strategies that require less day-to-day involvement, like long-term investing or swing trading. Conversely, if you can monitor the markets closely, day trading could become a viable option.

It's essential to factor in your level of expertise. Novice traders might benefit from simple strategies focusing on basic indicators and patterns before progressing to complex analyses. More experienced traders can explore sophisticated combinations of indicators and advanced chart patterns. Continuous education and practice, such as backtesting or demo trading, can help refine your skills as you progress.

Determine the tools you need to implement your trading plan effectively. Whether it's specific charting software, technical indicators, or automated trading bots, the right resources can support your personalised strategy. Keep track of what works well for you and be prepared to adapt; the tools that suit one trading strategy might not be ideal for another.

Developing a routine is an often overlooked aspect of personalisation. Setting aside dedicated time for market analysis, reviewing past trades, and planning for future trades can establish a disciplined approach. This routine should include regular breaks and downtime, preventing trader fatigue and maintaining a balanced lifestyle. Consistency is key, but flexibility to adjust for life's unpredictability is equally vital.

As you refine your crypto trading plan, ensure it reflects an understanding of market psychology and the influence of human behaviour on price movements. Recognise the role of emotions such as fear and greed in decision-making. Techniques from the chapter on trading psychology, like setting predefined rules for entering and exiting trades, can minimise emotional interference.

Risk management should be woven into every component of your trading plan. Strategies like setting stop-loss orders or diversifying portfolios are standard, but customisation involves determining these based on your unique criteria. Assessing the risk-reward ratio of potential trades will help align your strategies with your financial goals and risk appetite.

Additionally, the dynamic nature of the crypto market means it's critical to remain adaptable. Regularly review and adjust your plan. Market conditions, personal circumstances, and individual goals can shift, necessitating changes to your strategies. Plan reviews should be systematic but flexible enough to accommodate unforeseen developments swiftly.

Community engagement can also play a role in personalising your trading plan. Engage with forums, webinars, and social networks specific to crypto trading. These platforms provide valuable insights and perspectives. However, filtering this information is crucial to avoid the noise and focus on data that aligns with your strategy.

Documenting your trading journey is another layer of personalisation that's beneficial over the long term. Maintain a trading journal to record the rationale behind each trade, the results, and your emotional state at the time. Reflecting on this information can reveal patterns in your trading behaviour, highlighting areas for improvement.

A personalised trading plan stands to evolve by integrating technology and staying abreast of emerging trends. As the crypto landscape changes, so should your approach. Continual learning and adaptation ensure you remain resilient and capable of seizing new opportunities.

In conclusion, customising your crypto trading plan is an empowering process that aligns trading strategies with personal aspirations and circumstances. While the foundation of the plan is built on core trading principles, its success lies in how well it echoes your unique financial vision. By committing to education, practice, and adaptation, you'll forge a path to achieving your trading objectives in the ever-evolving world of crypto.

Chapter 19: Day Trading vs. Long-Term Investing in Crypto

In the world of crypto, the decision between day trading and long-term investing is akin to choosing between a fast-paced sprint and a measured marathon, each with its distinct rhythm and challenges. Day trading demands quick reflexes, a keen eye for fleeting patterns, and the ability to make rapid decisions that could yield substantial short-term gains. Meanwhile, the long-term approach, akin to patiently tending a garden, requires an unflinching belief in crypto's potential and an ability to weather the market's often tumultuous storms in pursuit of future growth. The key lies not only in understanding the mechanics of each strategy but also in aligning them with your personal goals, risk tolerance, and, crucially, the time you can commit to analysing these volatile digital assets. This chapter will guide you through the nuances of each approach, empowering you to choose the path that dovetails most harmoniously with your trading aspirations and lifestyle.

Comparing Day Trading and Long-Term Investing

In the rapidly evolving world of crypto, choosing between day trading and long-term investing often feels like picking a path through an unpredictable jungle. Each approach offers unique rewards and challenges, making the choice largely dependent on one's personal goals, risk tolerance, and lifestyle preferences.

While both strategies aim to reap financial benefits, they do so through remarkably different philosophies and techniques.

Day trading is akin to being in the thick of the action on a daily basis. It involves buying and selling crypto assets within a single trading day, often multiple times. The essence of this approach is to capture small price movements that can be capitalized on for profit. Day traders rely heavily on technical analysis tools, charts, and a robust understanding of market signals to make swift, informed decisions. This dynamic approach demands constant vigilance, quick reflexes, and the ability to maintain a cool head under pressure.

The allure of day trading lies in its potential for high returns on a daily basis, but it's not without its risks. Market volatility, while an ally in potential profits, can also be a formidable adversary leading to substantial losses if not managed carefully. It requires not only a comprehensive understanding of technical indicators but also a keen sense of timing and the ability to act decisively in volatile environments. There's excitement in the rapid pace and immediate feedback, yet this adrenaline-charged environment isn't suited for everyone.

Conversely, long-term investing in crypto is about seeing the bigger picture and is often compared to planting seeds with the expectation of eventual harvests. This approach requires patience and a strategic vision, as it involves holding assets for extended periods, often years. Instead of aiming for quick profits through rapid trades, long-term investors focus on the underlying fundamentals of a crypto asset and its future potential. This means thorough research into project viability, team capabilities, market adoption, and technology.

The strength of long-term investing lies in mitigating short-term volatility and capitalizing on the compound growth of assets over time. Investors in this category often experience less stress compared to day traders since they're not concerned with daily price fluctuations. Instead, they're in it for the long haul, banking on the belief that the asset will appreciate over time due to broader market trends or technological breakthroughs.

Yet, long-term investing is not an entirely passive process. Successful long-term investors stay informed about market trends, regulatory changes, and technological developments that could impact their holdings. They're prepared to adapt strategies as the market evolves, making informed decisions about when to hold, sell, or buy more. Patience is key, as is the trust in their due diligence and initial assessment of the investment's potential.

Comparing these two strategies often brings to light the critical elements of risk tolerance and personal preference. Day trading may suit individuals who thrive on daily challenges and can devote significant time to watching the markets. It offers the thrill of quick results but also demands the emotional resilience to endure losses and maintain focus in a highly competitive environment. Moreover, it necessitates a strategy that includes effective risk management tools to prevent significant capital erosion.

On the flip side, long-term investing could be the preferred route for those who have a stable financial base and wish to grow their wealth gradually with less active engagement. It appeals to individuals who favor a more hands-off approach, trusting in the power of compound interest and market growth. This method is particularly advantageous for those who can withstand market downturns while retaining confidence that the value of their assets will ultimately rise.

For those torn between these approaches, hybrid strategies might offer a balanced path. Combining elements of both day trading and long-term investing, individuals can allocate portions of their portfolio to active trading for near-term gains and another to longer-term investments for sustained growth. This blend leverages the advantages of both strategies while potentially offsetting the risks associated with each. By diversifying tactics, one can align their overall strategy with individual financial goals and risk appetite.

Ultimately, the decision between day trading and long-term investing should align with your personal circumstances and financial objectives. Are you prepared to dedicate the time and energy required for day trading? Does the appeal of potentially high stakes trade-offs resonate with your financial aspirations? Or do you prefer the gradual, albeit often slower, journey of long-term investment that demands patience and a forward-thinking perspective?

Perhaps, the choice need not be one or the other. Many seasoned traders and investors advocate for learning through experience. By experimenting with both strategies in small, measured ways, you can gain insight into your strengths, weaknesses, and preferences. Allow your experiences to guide you towards a strategy that complements both your lifestyle and ambitions, ultimately enabling you to navigate the crypto landscape with confidence.

Whether you choose the high-octane world of day trading or the patient road of long-term investing, the key is continuous learning and adaptation. The crypto world is ever-evolving, with new opportunities and challenges around every corner. Equip yourself with the right knowledge, tools, and mindset, and you can stand ready to craft a financial journey that's as rewarding as it is enlightening.

Choosing the Right Approach for You

In the thrilling yet intricate world of crypto trading and investing, one of the pivotal decisions you'll face is choosing between day trading and long-term investing. Each approach has its own set of demands, risks, and rewards, and the choice hinges largely on your personal goals, resources, and risk tolerance.

Day trading in crypto is akin to a fast-paced chess game where every move counts and the stakes are high. It's a domain where traders capitalize on short-term price movements, often engaging in multiple trades within a single day. This approach requires a keen eye on market charts, a deep understanding of technical analysis, and the agility to act swiftly.

Conversely, long-term investing is a strategy shaped by patience and foresight. It's akin to planting a tree, nurturing it over time, and watching it grow. Long-term investors typically hold crypto assets for months or even years, based on the belief in the potential of the underlying technology and market growth.

But how do you decide which path suits you best? Let's delve into several factors that should guide your decision-making process.

Your Time Commitment: Day trading demands a significant amount of time dedicated to watching market fluctuations and conducting continual analysis. If you're someone with a flexible schedule who thrives in high-pressure environments, this approach might suit you. Long-term investing, on the other hand, requires less frequent monitoring, making it a viable option for those juggling other commitments.

Risk Tolerance: How comfortable are you with the possibility of loss? Day trading involves higher risk due to the volatile nature of the crypto market. Price swings can be extreme and rapid, which can result in both substantial profits and substantial losses in a matter of hours. Long-term investing usually rides out short-term volatility in favour of potentially more stable long-term gains.

Market Knowledge and Technical Skills: Day traders need to be adept at technical analysis and must have a good grasp of trading platforms and tools. As you'll be making rapid decisions, the ability to interpret indicators and trends accurately is crucial. Long-term investors benefit more from fundamental analysis—evaluating the potential of crypto projects, tech viability, and market trends over time.

Emotional Resilience: Trading of any kind is a psychological game. Day trading requires significant emotional resilience since prices can fluctuate dramatically in minutes or even seconds. Your ability to remain calm under pressure and stick to your strategy without succumbing to emotional trading is vital. Long-term investors often face the test of patience and the pressure of holding through market downturns without panic selling.

Consider the resources at your disposal. For day trading, you'll need not only time but also technological tools and perhaps a mentor or community to help you refine your skills. Many successful day traders benefit from having a dedicated trading setup with multiple monitors and high-speed internet to track multiple indicators simultaneously.

Your financial situation and liquidity are also critical. Day trading may require working capital that you can afford to risk and possibly lose. These traders often utilise leverage to amplify their positions, which significantly increases both potential rewards and risks. Long-term investors, in contrast, might be more focused on accumulating holdings over time, employing a dollar-cost averaging strategy to mitigate market volatility and build wealth gradually.

Moreover, understanding your financial goals can steer you towards the right path. Are you seeking rapid financial gains and are prepared for the associated risks? Day trading might align with your ambitions. Alternatively, if you aim to build a portfolio with an eye towards future growth, consider long-term investing.

Never underestimate the importance of learning and adapting. Whichever path you choose, the crypto landscape changes rapidly, and staying informed and flexible will be essential. For day traders, this might mean continuous education on new indicators and market trends. For long-term investors, it may involve keeping abreast of technological advancements and regulatory changes affecting crypto.

It's also worth noting that you don't have to commit exclusively to one approach. Some traders diversify by allocating a portion of their portfolio to long-term strategies while still engaging in day trading to capitalise on short-term opportunities. This hybrid approach can balance potential gains with risk management, although it does require careful planning and discipline.

Ultimately, the path you choose should resonate with your lifestyle, goals, and financial circumstances. Both strategies offer distinct journeys with their own challenges and triumphs. By understanding your preferences and leveraging your strengths, you can chart a course that not only aligns with your objectives but also brings you fulfilment and success in the dynamic world of crypto trading and investing.

Chapter 20:

Case Studies of Successful Crypto Trades

Peering into the journeys of some triumphant crypto traders can reveal the practical applications of techniques that often appear abstract or theoretical. As the gloom of uncertainty sometimes clouds the crypto landscape, strategically devised actions—underpinned by sound analysis and a smidge of intuition—set apart successful traders. Consider a trader who navigated the volatile tides of Bitcoin during a bear market by leveraging Fibonacci retracement and volume analysis, capitalising on a carefully timed entry to secure significant returns. Another instance is the methodical employment of RSI divergences that allowed an insightful trader to anticipate reversals in Ethereum's price, making measured decisions that cushioned risks while amplifying profits. These case studies don't serve as prescriptive blueprints but rather illustrate how astute analyses, imbibed with a well-honed sense of timing and discipline, can convert knowledge into tangible success. Drawing lessons from such rich experiences equips aspiring traders with the mindset to see the bigger picture and seize opportunities with confidence and finesse.

Learning from Past Successes

Learning from the triumphs of previous crypto trades marks a pivotal approach in refining your trading strategy. When delving into successful trades, it's not only about celebrating the gain but, more importantly, dissecting the path taken to achieve them, gaining insights that bring clarity to the often unpredictable world of crypto markets.

One of the first steps in learning from successful trades is identifying the conditions that led to their success. Was it a surge in market sentiment, a brand-new technological innovation, or perhaps a timely tweet from a crypto influencer? Acknowledging these factors helps you understand what to watch for in future trades, providing a compass for navigating the market's ebbs and flows. Through an analytical approach, you can replicate these moments when similar circumstances arise again.

Alongside examining market conditions, revisiting the technical analysis tools you employed during successful trades can offer invaluable lessons. For instance, did a specific chart pattern signal the right move, or was there a particular indicator that proved decisive? By analysing which tools worked effectively, and under what condition, you refine your strategy, making it robust and flexible enough to adapt to changing circumstances. This exploration forms a personal toolbox, diligently crafted through real-world experiences.

Furthermore, successful trades often reflect sound risk management strategies. Reviewing these instances will likely reveal that well-calculated risks were taken. Consider the questions that guided these decisions: Were stop-loss limits tightly set to mitigate potential losses? Was the decision to enter or exit a trade based on a balanced evaluation of risk versus reward? By examining the mechanics of your past trades, you learn to fortify your strategies against future market volatility, ensuring that risks are managed rather than avoided outright.

Beyond the technical aspects and market conditions, the role of trading psychology can't be understated. Success in crypto trading is as much about maintaining discipline and emotional control as it is about technical know-how. Ask yourself how emotional disposition played into past wins: Did patience allow you to hold onto a trade longer than might have been psychologically comfortable? Was there the confidence to follow through on a well-thought-out strategy despite external noise? Reflecting on these psychological aspects not only entrenches valuable habits but also reveals areas for improvement.

Continuous learning from past trades fosters a growth mindset — one that views every success not as a static endpoint but as a part of a continuous learning journey. This mindset encourages adaptability in the face of an ever-evolving market landscape. Armed with insights from your past, you cultivate adaptability, ensuring your approach remains dynamic and responsive to new information, trends, and technologies.

Another integral piece in drawing lessons from successful trades involves acknowledging the role of meaningful evaluation and honest self-reflection. Sometimes, a trade might succeed by sheer luck, but grasping why is critical. Was it luck due to timing, or was there something else at play that was not immediately apparent? This self-awareness allows you to separate skill from serendipity, laying the groundwork for sustained profitable strategies that are continually refined rather than relying on unpredictable luck.

Going deeper, collaboration with fellow traders often brings fresh insights that might go unnoticed in solitary reflection. Participate in community discussion forums, attend seminars, or even join trading groups. Engaging with diverse perspectives provides a wealth of knowledge, often illuminating blind spots or biases you were previously unaware of. Collective insight doesn't just reaffirm your strategies; it challenges and augments your understanding, adding a breadth of experience beyond what any single trader could accumulate alone.

In conclusion, learning from past successes in crypto trading isn't just about analysing charts or tracking performance metrics. It's a holistic process involving understanding market conditions, choosing the right tools, practising sound risk management, maintaining emotional discipline, fostering a continuous learning mindset, being self-aware, and embracing community wisdom. Through diligent reflection and action, past triumphs can become the foundation upon which future successes are built, intertwining experience with strategic foresight for a consistently rewarding trading journey.

Analysing Key Trades for Insight

Success in crypto trading is not just about executing trades, but understanding what makes a trade successful. Delving into key trades allows us to discern common patterns and strategies tied to positive outcomes. In this section, we'll explore case studies of successful crypto trades to extract valuable insights, uncovering the ingredients of profitability that can serve any aspiring trader well.

First, let's acknowledge the dynamism of the cryptocurrency market. Traders often succeed not merely through happenstance but by strategically reading the landscape. Consider how successful trades begin with thorough research and a sound strategy, founded upon both fundamental and technical analysis. These are the bedrock of informed trading decisions. For instance, understanding the intricacies of a project and its team can offer foresight into the cryptocurrency's potential for growth or decline, guiding entry and exit points effectively.

Let's take a closer look at a real-world example: the rapid rise of Bitcoin in late 2017. Traders who seized this opportunity successfully identified a prolonged, clear uptrend and leveraged it to their advantage. By recognising the increasing trading volumes and the overall market sentiment around Bitcoin, they elucidated the trend's strength and persisted in long positions. This wasn't just about instinct; it was a testament to the power of trend analysis and understanding the importance of momentum in price actions.

Another critical component is the role of support and resistance levels. Successful crypto traders have consistently used these levels to not only place trades but also to set stop losses and take profits, fundamentally limiting risk. A skilled trader would have identified key support levels during Bitcoin's boom, giving them confidence to continue holding even amidst fluctuations. Likewise, locating resistance levels aided in determining optimal points to take profit, ensuring gains were locked in before potential reversals.

Candlestick patterns also have a place in the toolbox of successful trades. Recognising patterns such as the bullish engulfing or the hammer can offer valuable hints about potential market direction changes. Traders who understood these patterns effectively positioned themselves for the subsequent price moves, timing their trades to maximise profitability while minimising false breakouts.

Volume analysis cannot be overlooked. Successful traders don't merely focus on price movements but also on trading volume, which provides essential context about the strength of a price movement. A surge in volume often corroborates the sustainability of a trend. For instance, during Ethereum's significant price rally in 2021, astute traders noticed a corresponding increase in volume, validating the trend's legitimacy and enabling them to ride the wave with confidence.

Risk management has equally been a hallmark of prosperous trading ventures. It's not just about maximising gains but protecting capital. Establishing a robust risk-reward ratio kept traders on the right side of the market even when unexpected volatility arose. In this way, they were not only prepared to exploit opportunities but also shielded against adverse movements.

Moreover, recognising the emotional and psychological aspects is critical. The mental fortitude of successful traders often sets them apart. Cultivating a mindset that balances discipline with flexibility aids in executing planned strategies without succumbing to fear or greed. This psychological mastery ensures that traders maintain their strategies even under market pressure, solidifying their resilience and consistency.

Backtesting strategies prior to live deployment has similarly contributed to perfected execution in trades. In essence, by simulating trades against historical data, traders can validate the effectiveness of their methodologies before capital is ever risked. This practice has illuminated vital tweaks in strategies, transforming them from theoretically sound to practically potent.

However, key trades aren't locked in the past—a constant evaluation and adaptation are required. Markets evolve, and so must strategies. Learning from past successful trades involves continuously refining techniques, integrating new tools, and staying abreast of technological advancements, all of which sustain profitability over time.

As we gather insights from these successfully executed trades, it becomes apparent that the convergence of discipline, analysis, and adaptive learning formulates a comprehensive blueprint for trading success. By weaving these elements together with personal insight and innovation, traders can craft a unique and effective approach that enhances their trading repertoire.

Every trade, especially those that succeed, holds lessons far richer than mere profit or loss figures. It's in these trades that crucial elements of market mechanics are unveiled, presenting an opportunity to continually build upon one's own foundation of trading acumen. Armed with these insights, any trader is better equipped to navigate the ever-volatile seas of cryptocurrency trading.

Chapter 21: Leveraging Crypto Trading Bots

As we've journeyed through the intricacies of crypto trading, it's time to delve into the world of automation—a modern trader's ally in the fast-paced crypto market. Leveraging crypto trading bots can revolutionise how traders navigate the volatile landscape by executing pre-set strategies swiftly and without emotion. These bots, akin to tireless digital assistants, are designed to monitor market conditions continuously, capitalising on opportunities that may elude human attention. While they're not a guaranteed path to riches, incorporating them into your trading arsenal can lead to enhanced efficiency and precision. Before diving into automated trading, it's crucial to evaluate the myriad of bot options available, ensuring they align with your trading goals and risk appetite. Mastering the art of bots involves meticulous strategy crafting and ongoing adjustments, transforming your trading approach from reactive to proactive, and potentially more profitable.

Introduction to Automated Trading

In the dynamic world of crypto trading, automation is fast becoming a game-changer. Gone are the days when traders were tethered to their screens, painstakingly trying to predict market movements through constant manual analysis. With the evolution of technology, automated trading has emerged as a powerful tool, providing traders with a means to execute orders at speeds and efficiency levels that far exceed human capabilities.

Automated trading, sometimes referred to as algorithmic trading, leverages computer programs to analyse market data and execute trades based on pre-defined parameters. These scripts, often known as trading bots, are designed to perform tasks that would be difficult, if not impossible, for a human to manage unassisted. Imagine trying to keep track of multiple currency pairs, continuously monitoring for the slightest of market shifts, and instantly executing trades when certain conditions are met. This is where automation steps in.

The appeal of using trading bots lies in their ability to minimise human errors and emotions. Many traders have, in the heat of the moment, made impulsive decisions that led to losses. An automated system, unaffected by the psychological pitfalls of fear and greed, executes trades purely based on data-driven criteria. This objectivity often results in more disciplined and consistent trading outcomes.

Moreover, the value of automated trading extends beyond execution speed and efficiency. It also brings about the possibility of backtesting strategies on historical data. By doing so, traders can verify the viability of their strategies before risking capital. This capacity to assess and refine strategies through backtesting is a significant advantage, enabling traders to hone their approaches continually without incurring real-world losses.

Of course, setting up an automated trading system isn't merely about programming a bot and letting it run wild. It requires a well-thought-out strategy and thorough understanding of market dynamics. A trading bot is only as effective as the strategy it's based on. Traders must invest time in building and refining strategies that align with their trading objectives and risk tolerance.

It's critical to realise that automated trading doesn't remove every risk. Market conditions can change abruptly, and automated systems, while fast, might not always adapt quickly enough to sudden shifts if they're based on static rules. Hence, regular monitoring and updates to the system are essential. This keeps the strategies relevant and pertinent to the current market climate.

Getting started with automated trading in the crypto market can be an exhilarating yet daunting experience. There are myriad options available, each offering distinct features and capabilities. Some systems come with complex algorithms and require in-depth programming knowledge, while others are more user-friendly, aimed at beginners. These systems can deliver robust solutions with tailored features to suit various trading styles and objectives.

For traders who aren't comfortable developing their bots from scratch, there are platforms and services that offer ready-made bots. These options often provide code-free interfaces, allowing traders to set parameters through a simple web-based dashboard. It’s an inviting approach for those who are new to the concept yet wish to explore automation.

Security remains a primary concern when using automated trading systems. Entrusting a bot with access to one's trading account can be risky. Hence, ensuring that bot services are reputable and secure is crucial. Opt for platforms that offer robust security features and verify their credibility through community reviews and regulatory compliance records.

In conclusion, incorporating automated trading into your crypto trading strategy can be a wise decision. It combines speed, precision, and the ability to handle multiple trades with ease—a trifecta that can't be matched by manual trading alone. As with any tool, its effectiveness is ultimately decided by how it’s used. Understand the mechanics, develop smart strategies, and continually iterate on them. With these practices, automated trading can significantly elevate your trading game and set you on a path to achieving your trading goals.

Evaluating Trading Bot Options

When the dynamic world of cryptocurrency trading beckons, the allure of technology driven by crypto trading bots becomes irresistible for many traders and investors. These bots offer an opportunity to automate trading strategies and execute trades with precision and speed that would be challenging to achieve manually. But like any tool, the effectiveness of a trading bot depends on how it's chosen and used.

First and foremost, identifying the right trading bot starts with understanding your personal trading goals. Are you looking to actively day trade, or is a long-term investment strategy more your speed? Your strategy will guide the choice of bot features you need to focus on. Each bot has unique offerings – some excel in speculative trading with aggressive high-frequency algorithms, while others might be tailored to long-term holding with minimal interventions.

The multitude of options can be overwhelming, but this is where evaluation becomes key. Begin by looking at the bot's track record. Has it consistently performed well in varying market conditions? A robust trading bot will have a proven history of performing in both bullish and bearish cycles. If the bot is relatively new, examine its underlying technology and the experience of its developers.

Security should be at the forefront when evaluating trading bots, especially in the volatile world of cryptocurrency. Cryptocurrency exchanges are prime targets for hackers, making security considerations paramount. A reliable trading bot should offer strong encryption and never require access to your API keys in a way that compromises their security. Look for bots that have been audited for security, where possible, and check user reviews for any past incidents or breaches.

Next on your checklist should be the bot's compatibility with exchanges. Not all bots work seamlessly with every trading platform, and your choice will often be limited by your preferred exchanges. Some bots are designed for a specific platform while others are more versatile, supporting multiple exchanges. Ensure your trading bot works with the exchanges you frequently use, and that it can operate effectively across them.

Customisability is another crucial factor. A trading bot should align well with your trading strategy. Seek out bots that offer customisable parameters, allowing you to tweak and adjust strategies as needed. This flexibility can be especially useful in adapting to market shifts. Moreover, a bot with backtesting features is a huge advantage, as it allows you to test strategies on historical data before implementing them live, helping to avoid costly mistakes.

While evaluating the technical prowess of trading bots, also take into account customer support and community engagement. The best technologies sometimes fall short if support is lacking. Good customer service can be the difference when you're troubleshooting issues in the midst of a volatile market. Additionally, an active community of users can serve as a valuable resource for advice and troubleshooting tips. Bots with strong community support often have forums, chat groups, or other platforms where users can share insights and strategies.

It's also wise to consider the bot's cost versus its potential benefit. Trading bots can range from free, basic models to monthly subscription-based services with advanced features. While free options might be tempting, they often come with limitations that could affect performance. Weigh the cost against the features offered and determine if the potential returns justify the expense. This calculation should also factor in your risk tolerance and expected trading volume.

Another subtle yet important consideration involves the legal and regulatory landscape. Different countries have diverse regulations when it comes to automated trading and crypto assets. Before settling on a bot, ensure its operations are compliant with the legal guidelines of your jurisdiction. This diligence will save you from potential legal troubles down the line and ensure smooth operation.

As you assess these elements, always keep your goals and available resources in mind. There's no one-size-fits-all solution, and the right trading bot for one trader might not suit another. It's crucial to perform due diligence and possibly even consult with other crypto traders. Peer recommendations and shared experiences can lead you to the best choice for your circumstances.

The right bot, chosen carefully, can transform your trading experience, offering not only efficiency and speed but also opening up new opportunities for profit. As technology evolves, these tools will become increasingly sophisticated, making the evaluation process even more essential. Equip yourself with knowledge, remain adaptable, and use these tools judiciously toward your trading success.

Chapter 22: Evaluating Crypto Market News and Impact

Navigating the rapidly evolving landscape of crypto requires a keen eye for news that can sway market sentiment in an instant. In this chapter, we'll dive into the art of deciphering the barrage of crypto news, distinguishing between the din of market noise and truly valuable insights that can shape trading decisions. It's about honing in on which pieces of information wield real influence, driving price action and market trends. Being able to discern market logic from hype is essential; understanding how upcoming network upgrades, regulatory announcements, or institutional adoptions can signal pivotal shifts empowers traders. Keep in mind that not all news is created equal, and recognising the catalysts with genuine impact can make the difference between a well-placed trade and a miscalculated risk. In embracing this skill, you'll learn to filter out the distractions, focusing on developments that truly matter, thus refining your strategy and ultimately finding those edges in the crypto world where clarity often seems elusive.

Understanding Market News Influence

In the fast-paced and ever-evolving world of cryptocurrency, news can be a driving force capable of influencing market behaviour in the blink of an eye. An insightful trader knows that news isn't just information—it's a catalyst that can prompt significant price swings. In mastering crypto market analysis, understanding how to interpret market news becomes not only a skill but a necessity. This chapter will equip you with the tools to discern the true impact of news, helping you distinguish between headline noise and information that could shape your trading strategies.

Crypto markets are highly sensitive to news due to their nascent nature and speculative aspects. News related to regulations, technological advancements, outages, or security breaches can trigger swift changes in the market, leading to volatility. For instance, a government announcing new regulations can cause panic selling or encourage buying, depending on the context and perceived impact. Understanding this dynamic requires a keen sense of observation and anticipation, enabling traders to navigate these waters with enhanced foresight.

A vital part of gauging news influence is recognising the source and credibility. Trusted financial news outlets, blockchain developers' announcements, or words from influential figures in the crypto space can carry different weights. It's important for traders to discern whether the news is coming from a credible source or is a speculation-driven narrative. Having a network of reliable information sources ensures that you're informed by facts rather than fiction, thus minimising reactionary decision-making.

It's crucial to differentiate between short-term noise and long-term impact. Short-term noise often involves news that spikes interest and price activity but doesn’t lead to lasting changes or trends. Conversely, news indicating a fundamental shift, like a major company adopting blockchain technology, could herald opportunities for long-term strategic positioning. Traders should evaluate how the news fits into broader market trends or innovations, understanding that some information may have a temporal market effect.

Emotional management is an underrated, yet pivotal aspect when dealing with market news. The crypto landscape moves rapidly, and news, whether it's positive or negative, can trigger emotional responses. Traders must develop the skill to control these reactions, ensuring decisions are based on analysis rather than impulse. Cultivating a calm and calculated approach prevents rash decisions that could harm your portfolio.

Considering how the global context influences the market is another critical element. The interconnectedness of global economies means that an event in one part of the world can ripple through the crypto markets. Economic downturns, international conflicts, or technological breakthroughs can provoke widespread market changes. Traders must not only focus on the crypto-specific news but also keep a close watch on broader economic indicators that could indirectly affect the crypto markets.

Analysing past market reactions to news can provide invaluable insights. Looking back at historical instances where major news impacted the cryptocurrency markets can help identify patterns or tendencies in market behaviour. For example, understanding how past regulatory announcements influenced specific crypto assets might help predict future market reactions. Learning from history doesn't provide guaranteed outcomes but can enhance a trader's ability to anticipate market movements.

Furthermore, it's essential to appreciate the role of social media in shaping market sentiment. Platforms like Twitter and Reddit can amplify voices that influence market perceptions and trends. While these platforms democratise information dissemination, they also pose the risk of misinformation. Traders should critically assess the validity of social media claims, cross-checking with verified sources to avoid falling into traps of hype or misinformation.

As you become more adept at understanding market news, leveraging this knowledge can help fine-tune your trading strategies. Identifying whether news will lead to long-term changes or is merely a temporary blip can help determine the appropriate reaction—be it immediate action or strategic patience. This discernment is where seasoned traders distinguish themselves from the novice, capitalising on information that others may overlook or misinterpret.

In conclusion, understanding market news influence is not just about digesting headlines—it's about interpreting the undercurrents of information that can drive the crypto markets. By developing a framework for analysing news sources, controlling emotional reactions, and learning from past market responses, traders can effectively integrate this knowledge into their trading strategies. Armed with these skills, you'll be well-positioned to make informed decisions that align with your trading objectives, ultimately elevating your ability to navigate the crypto market's vibrant and volatile waters. Remember, in the world of crypto trading, information is power, and the ability to interpret that information wisely is the key to unlocking your trading potential.

Distinguishing Between Noise and Valuable Information

The sheer volume of information bombarding crypto traders daily is staggering. With the relentless stream of news, tweets, forums, and market analysis, the crypto market can feel like a cacophony of noise. Yet, within this din lies the crucial task of distinguishing what's valuable from what's mere distraction. This skill is paramount for any trader aspiring to navigate the volatile waters of cryptocurrency trading successfully.

Identifying quality information begins with understanding the sources. In the crypto world, the legitimacy and trustworthiness of information are often inextricably linked to the reputation of its source. Established financial publications, reputable crypto news sites, and verified accounts of industry leaders typically offer valuable insights. In contrast, unverified social media posts and obscure websites can sometimes spread misinformation or hype, which can mislead traders into making hasty decisions.

Furthermore, traders must learn to question the timing and context of the information. Market-moving news often follows patterns or events, such as updates on regulatory decisions, technological advancements, or major institutional investments. Such events provide clarity amidst the noise, highlighting shifts in market sentiment that are worth noting. Learning to spot these patterns and understand their implications is a skill honed over time and experience.

Emotion plays a pivotal role in how information is perceived, often creating an additional layer of noise. FOMO (fear of missing out) and FUD (fear, uncertainty, and doubt) are prevalent emotions that can skew a trader's judgment. These emotional responses can amplify the noise, as traders may react impulsively to market fluctuations or speculative rumours. Building emotional resilience and maintaining a disciplined approach to trading is crucial in staying focused on valuable information.

Analysing the content's depth and detail is another essential strategy. Genuine insights often delve deeper into the context, providing data-backed analysis and logical reasoning. In contrast, superficial news or exaggerated headlines designed to grab attention can often be misleading. Traders should prioritize information that offers comprehensive analysis and aligns with their trading goals and strategies.

Additionally, critical thinking is indispensable when evaluating information. This involves questioning the assumptions behind the headlines, being wary of biases in analysis, and understanding the potential motivations behind sensational news. Often, the most valuable insights stem from a balanced approach that considers differing viewpoints and corroborates data across multiple reliable sources.

Automation and technology can also play a supportive role in filtering information. Modern trading platforms and analytical tools offer news filters, sentiment analysis, and customizable alerts tailored to a trader's specific interests. These tools can streamline the process of identifying potentially valuable information, ensuring traders remain informed without becoming overwhelmed.

Lastly, creating a structured routine for information consumption can prevent overload. Setting specific times for digesting market updates, perhaps at the beginning or end of trading sessions, can maintain focus and discipline. This routine ensures traders have the mental bandwidth to deeply engage with information rather than reacting impulsively to every new development.

As traders develop the skill to distinguish between noise and valuable information, they empower themselves to make more informed and measured decisions. This discernment is a crucial component of successful trading strategies, fostered by experience, patience, and a disciplined approach to market analysis. The journey to mastering crypto markets is rife with distractions, yet those who learn to tune out the noise and focus on what truly matters will likely find greater success and resilience in their trading endeavors.

Chapter 23: Avoiding Common Crypto Trading Pitfalls

Embarking on a crypto trading journey can be thrilling and, at times, overwhelming, given the market's volatile nature. Understanding common pitfalls can save you from financial mishaps and emotional turmoil. Many traders fall into the trap of emotional decisions, often swayed by fear of missing out or panic selling during price drops. A disciplined approach, guided by consistent strategy and proper risk management, can mitigate such impulsive reactions. Also, over-reliance on singular indicators without considering the broader market context can lead to misguided trades. Diversifying your strategies and maintaining a balanced view of both technical and fundamental analyses are essential in avoiding tunnel vision. Moreover, neglecting ongoing education in this fast-evolving space can leave you vulnerable to outdated practices. Embrace a continuous learning mindset, and you'll find yourself better equipped to navigate the complexities of crypto trading with confidence.

Identifying Common Mistakes

Embarking on a journey through the dynamic world of crypto trading is no small feat. With countless opportunities and an equal number of potential pitfalls, traders must navigate their strategies with precision and insight. Identifying common mistakes forms a crucial part of this learning curve, as understanding where others have faltered can often illuminate the path to success.

A prevalent mistake among budding traders is letting emotions dictate their trading decisions. It's all too easy to see excitement in the green candlesticks of a bullish market or despair in the red of a bearish downturn. However, trading based on emotions rather than research and analysis leads to hasty decisions that often result in losses. Successful traders learn to detach their feelings from their trades, ensuring decisions are made using comprehensive data and clearly set objectives, not spur-of-the-moment impulses.

Overtrading is another frequent misstep. With all the thrill the crypto market offers, traders often feel the compulsion to make trades constantly, thinking more trades equate to more profits. In reality, trading too frequently dilutes focus and typically racks up transaction fees, eating into potential profits. Experienced traders understand the importance of being selective and patient, waiting for high-quality setups rather than chasing every price movement.

Failing to conduct proper research before entering trades tends to be a severe oversight. The volatility and complexity of cryptocurrencies mean that a robust understanding of the market landscape is indispensable. Jumping into trades without thorough due diligence or trusting unreliable information sources sets traders up for failure. Scrutinising market indicators, evaluating the underlying projects, and absorbing credible industry news are imperative to crafting informed and strategic trades.

Another mistake that cripples many is ignoring a proper risk management strategy. Enthused by the potential for high returns, traders often risk more than they can afford to lose, leaving them vulnerable should the market move against their positions. Establishing stop-loss orders, diversifying investment portfolios, and calculating position sizes according to risk tolerance are non-negotiables for maintaining a sustainable trading approach.

Traders often find themselves paralysed by indecision, particularly newer entrants. The plethora of information and signals can be overwhelming, causing analysis paralysis where too much information leads to inaction. Delegating priority to key indicators and adhering to a solid trading plan, without obsessing over every minute detail, helps in building the confidence needed for decisive trading actions.

Next, let's discuss neglecting the importance of learning from past trades, a habit that can impede growth in any trader's career. Without examining what went right and what went wrong, traders miss a crucial opportunity to refine their strategies. Keeping a trading journal and regular backtesting allow for critical introspection. This saves traders from repeating mistakes and enables them to refine methods that are working successfully.

The lack of a clear exit strategy is a common mistake that can lead to significant setbacks. Traders often focus solely on entry points and neglect planning their exits, leading to losses or diminished gains. Knowing when to exit is just as crucial as entry, requiring traders to establish profit targets and stop-loss levels before initiating trades. A well-thought-out exit plan ensures traders maximise profits and mitigate losses effectively.

Many traders slip into the mistake of short-term focus at the expense of a broader perspective. The thrill of day-to-day market swings can detract from understanding the bigger picture trends and long-term strategies. Aligning short-term decisions with long-term goals is essential for sustained success in the volatile crypto space. Cultivating a balanced perspective enables traders to navigate volatile markets with resilience and strategic foresight.

While avoiding these common mistakes won't guarantee success, it significantly increases the odds of crafting a winning strategy. Learning from these pitfalls empowers traders to forge a disciplined, informed approach to the crypto market, honing the skills necessary for calculated risk-taking. The path to becoming a proficient trader isn't devoid of errors, but recognising and rectifying these mistakes is the hallmark of a successful trading mindset.

Strategies to Avoid Trading Errors

Success in the realm of crypto trading isn't solely about seizing opportunities; it's also about sidestepping potential pitfalls. Crafting effective strategies to avoid trading errors can be your armour against unnecessary losses. Let's dive into those strategies, beginning with a comprehensive understanding of your chosen market. For starters, an in-depth market analysis forms the backbone of any trading decision. Before placing any trade, whether it's short-term or long-term, take the time to thoroughly research market conditions and trends. This diligence isn't just about spotting potential gains; it's about recognising unfavourable climates that might necessitate sitting on the sidelines until conditions improve.

Building a strong foundational knowledge of crypto assets is another crucial strategy. Understand what you're investing in beyond the ticker symbol. Ask questions: What's the project's vision? Who are the developers, and what's their track record? Scrutinise the fundamentals, as they are the compass that will guide your trading strategy. In doing so, you empower yourself to make informed decisions, minimising the risk of errors stemming from inadequate research or hype-driven purchases.

Diversification is another key component to consider. Putting all your eggs in one basket can expose you to greater risk. Instead, consider a diversified portfolio to spread risk. Allocating your investments across various assets can buffer against market volatility and result in a more balanced risk profile. However, diversification needs to be strategic. Blindly scattering investments without thorough research or a clear understanding of each asset's characteristics might lead to the very traps you're trying to avoid.

When deploying strategies, the role of meticulous risk management cannot be overstressed. Implementing a robust risk management plan involves setting clear stop-loss and take-profit limits. These limits act as a safety net, ensuring that you're never risking more than you can afford to lose. By defining your risk-reward ratio upfront, you discipline your trading habits, making emotional reactions less likely to derail your plans. Emotion-driven trading can lead to significant mistakes, underscoring the importance of having well-defined mechanisms to manage risk.

Navigating emotional impulses—often a trader's Achilles' heel—requires a high level of self-awareness and emotional discipline. You need to tackle the psychological aspects of trading head-on by cultivating a resilient mindset. This involves recognising the emotional triggers that might lead to rash decisions, like the urge to chase losses or the fear of missing out on a sudden price surge. By understanding your psychological tendencies, you can develop strategies to stay focused on logic and analysis rather than emotions.

Trading plans provide yet another vital fail-safe. Creating a well-structured trading plan is not just academic; it's your blueprint for action. It's a detailed document outlining trading objectives, market analysis frameworks, entry and exit strategies, and risk parameters. A solid plan helps maintain discipline and ensures consistency in executing tasks. More importantly, it serves as a reference to measure your progress, evaluate performance, and make necessary adjustments.

The significance of backtesting to evaluate the effectiveness of your strategies cannot be overemphasised. Before applying any strategy in the live market, it's advisable to backtest it using historical data. This process will reveal the probable outcomes and align your expectations with reality. By simulating trades, you can refine your methodology and identify potential flaws, allowing you to adjust before committing real capital. Remember, a strategy that hasn't been thoroughly vetted through backtesting might have unseen weaknesses that could contribute to trading errors.

Adopting a learning mindset is also part and parcel of avoiding trading mistakes. Rather than viewing errors as setbacks, interpret them as learning opportunities. Maintain a journal to document trades, from initial thoughts and analysis to the outcome and emotions involved. This practice promotes continuous learning, allowing you to spot patterns of error and subtle biases that might influence your decision-making. The more insights you gather from past mistakes, the better prepared you are to avoid them in the future.

Lastly, long-term success in crypto trading often hinges on flexibility and adaptability. The crypto market is notoriously volatile and ever-evolving. Thus, the ability to pivot strategies based on changing market conditions is essential. Remain open to new information and be willing to adjust your strategies as required. Staunch rigidity in your approach can make you susceptible to decisional errors. Stay informed, remain adaptable, and consistently align your strategies with the current market landscape to maximise your potential for consistent, error-free trading.

In conclusion, developing sophisticated strategies that avoid trading errors is about more than knowledge; it requires disciplined execution. Adopt a holistic approach encompassing market understanding, emotional discipline, strategic planning, and persistent evaluation. By committing to these principles, you pave the way towards a successful and rewarding crypto trading experience.

Chapter 24: Bridging the Gap: Traditional Markets vs. Crypto

The dynamic realm of crypto trading often presents a steep learning curve, especially for those seasoned in traditional markets. Yet, the core principles of understanding market structure and methodologies often remain the same, providing a valuable bridge for transitioning traders. It's crucial to appreciate that while price movements in equities and bonds rely on historical financial data and predictable cycles, crypto markets pivot on blockchain innovations, decentralisation, and rapidly changing sentiment. For aspiring crypto traders, deciphering these nuances can be transformative. By leveraging your knowledge from traditional trading, such as interpreting technical indicators and managing risk, and adapting it to the volatile and fast-paced landscape of cryptocurrencies, you can enhance your trading prowess. In this way, the gap between these markets isn't a chasm but a pathway filled with opportunities for those ready to innovate and adapt.

Recognising Differences and Similarities

Navigating the realms of traditional markets and the ever-evolving crypto landscape can feel like moving between two distinct worlds. Yet, these worlds aren't as divergent as they might initially appear. Both traditional and crypto markets share foundational principles that are essential for any trader aiming for success. Understanding these similarities can be as valuable as recognising the differences when crafting your trading strategies.

In traditional markets, instruments like stocks and bonds are backed by tangible assets or enterprise value. The crypto market, on the other hand, often revolves around digital currencies that lack physical form. This core difference renders cryptocurrency somewhat elusive, making the market inherently more volatile but brimming with opportunities for those who can decode its patterns. It's a dance of understanding the tangible versus the digital, the predictable against the disruptive.

Both traditional and crypto traders rely heavily on data to drive their decisions. Technical analysis, for instance, plays a pivotal role in both landscapes. Charts reflect human psychology—they reveal trader sentiment, predict potential outcomes, and help reduce risk. Learning to interpret price action, through candlesticks and trendlines, draws a significant parallel between these two markets. A trader skilled in reading stock charts will find familiar territory when assessing crypto charts, even if the volatility faces a steeper gradient.

One noteworthy difference lies in the concept of market hours. Traditional markets are tied to the nine-to-five business model, with trading replicating those clocked hours. Crypto, however, never sleeps. It's a 24/7 affair without borders, without downtime. This round-the-clock trading offers both flexibility and a constant barrage of data and analysis. Traders must, therefore, equip themselves to handle fluid market dynamics, adapting to the relentless pace of change.

Regulatory landscapes starkly contrast in these markets, too. Traditional financial markets operate under the watchful eyes of established authorities, providing a sense of security despite their occasional unpredictability. Crypto markets, by contrast, are held with a looser grip. Regulation here is a patchwork quilt, varied across different countries and regions, leading to uncertainty but also a sense of innovation unhampered by stringent controls.

Yet, the driving forces behind price movements often share striking similarities. Both markets respond to supply and demand dynamics, economic indicators, geopolitical tensions, and monetary policies. The ripple effects of an interest rate shift or a trade agreement can be felt across stocks and crypto alike. The skills required to navigate these economic indicators can translate well from one market to another, enabling savvy traders to pivot their strategies accordingly.

This crossover potential is mirrored in sentiment analysis. Just as stock market fluctuations may swing as a result of investor sentiment driven by economic news or company earnings, crypto enthusiast communities can fuel massive price shifts. It's a similar but amplified echo, where tweets or speculative buying on an altcoin can lead to dramatic swings. Harnessing sentiment requires a prudent eye, a grasp on social trends, and a knack for distinguishing substantive information from noise.

Technological advancements also act as a bridge between these two markets. Algorithm-driven trading, once a domain of stock exchanges, now finds a place in the crypto world. Trading bots use sophisticated algorithms to execute trades at speeds beyond human capabilities, and their application in crypto has grown exponentially. This similarity demonstrates how innovation permeates both domains, challenging traders to stay informed and adaptable.

Moreover, the fundamental analysis in traditional markets, which evaluates financial statements and industry positioning, finds a parallel in crypto. Here, prospective traders investigate blockchain projects, assessing whitepapers, team credibility, and community engagement. Though the metrics differ, the essence of a thorough evaluation remains constant: determining value and potential based on qualitative and quantitative insights.

Despite these parallels, there remains a unique ethos to crypto: decentralisation. The decentralisation mantra, intrinsic to blockchain technology, contrasts sharply with the hierarchical structures governing traditional markets. This ethos bestows more power upon individuals, fostering an ecosystem where innovation thrives unshackled by conventional norms. For those adept in traditional trading, this represents both a challenge and a liberation, requiring an openness to uncharted methods.

Transitioning skills between these markets means acknowledging their interwoven yet distinct nature. Time-tested strategies in stocks might not map seamlessly onto crypto due to its idiosyncrasies, yet, understanding market psychology and technical analysis certainly holds value across both domains. Ultimately, recognising the differences and similarities in traditional and crypto markets equips traders with a comprehensive toolkit, blending the old with the new to carve out a path to trading success.

Translating Traditional Market Skills to Crypto

For many seasoned investors, the conventional financial markets like stocks, bonds, and commodities have long been ingrained into their skill set and understanding. Moving into the dynamic and rapid world of cryptocurrency might appear daunting at first glance. However, the skills honed in traditional markets are not only transferable but can also offer a distinct advantage in the crypto trading arena.

At the heart of successful trading, be it stocks or crypto, lies the art and science of analysis. Investors versed in traditional markets often rely on a blend of fundamental and technical analysis to make informed decisions. These analytical skills, honed through years of watching market patterns, reading financial statements, and understanding economic indicators, have direct relevance in the world of crypto. For instance, traditional market traders are adept at recognising patterns in charts, and these skills directly translate to reading crypto price movements. Being able to spot trends or reversals early on is key to succeeding in both realms.

One key similarity between traditional markets and the crypto space is the emphasis on quantitative analysis. Experienced traders understand that backtesting strategies, analysing historical data, and scrutinising metrics are crucial steps in decision-making. The crypto market, volatile as it is, can greatly benefit from such measures. The skill of interpreting quantitative data, identifying relevant trading indicators, and making data-driven decisions plays a critical role in forecasting market movements and executing successful trades.

However, transitioning from traditional markets to crypto doesn't just involve direct skill translation, but also the adaptation of mindset and approach. The principles of trading psychology are universal and play a significant role in managing emotions, risk, and expectations. Experienced traders will recall times in traditional markets where emotion-driven decisions clouded judgment. With the inherently volatile nature of crypto, managing psychological biases and maintaining discipline remain just as crucial. In fact, the extensively volatile swings in crypto often magnify the need for emotional resilience and a cool head.

Furthermore, the understanding of market mechanics, such as liquidity and order flow, is another transferable skill. Markets operate on supply and demand fundamentals, regardless of the asset class. Skilled traders from traditional markets often have a keen eye for liquidity and volume trends. In crypto, these factors manifest through order book depth, trading volume, and spread analysis. Hence, identifying liquidity levels and volume spikes in crypto markets can be just as pivotal as it is in traditional ones, aiding in the timing of entries and exits.

Risk management is yet another area where seasoned traditional market traders can leverage their expertise in crypto. The core tenets of managing risk — such as position sizing, setting stop-loss levels, and diversifying portfolios — are just as applicable. In crypto, risk management must sometimes account for additional factors like exchange security risks or regulatory changes. Nevertheless, the fundamental strategies remain unchanged: limit your exposure and prepare for unforeseen market moves.

Seasoned traders are also adept at maintaining a balanced portfolio. This skill is valuable when venturing into the varied landscape of cryptocurrency. Just as a traditional investor wouldn't put all their money into a single stock, successful crypto traders distribute their investments across different coins and tokens. Balancing a portfolio in crypto means understanding not only the individual assets but also the overarching market cycles that can impact the entire crypto sphere.

While the tools and platforms might vary slightly, traditional market traders can adjust relatively easily to crypto trading platforms. Order types such as market orders, limit orders, and stop orders retain their functionality across markets. Additionally, an understanding of leverage and margin — tools often employed in traditional markets — can provide strategic advantages when used cautiously in crypto trading.

For those traders moving from stocks and bonds to crypto, adaptability is crucial. Being open to learning about blockchain technology, decentralised finance (DeFi), and the nuances of crypto regulation will empower traders from traditional markets to fully exploit their existing skills. These new concepts, while daunting, enrich one's trading arsenal when integrated with traditional knowledge, reinforcing the principle that a dynamic and informed trader is more likely to succeed.

In essence, traditional market skills offer a solid foundation upon which crypto trading strategies can be built. By recognising similarities, adapting to differences, and continuously learning, traders can bridge the gap effectively. As you move forward, remember that a seamless transition is not just about skills but also about embracing the transformative potential of cryptocurrency in today's financial world.

Chapter 25: Future Trends in Crypto Trading

As we venture into the future of crypto trading, the landscape promises to be shaped by a blend of technological advancements and evolving market dynamics. The continuous integration of artificial intelligence and machine learning algorithms is set to revolutionise how data is interpreted and trading strategies are formulated, giving traders unprecedented tools to predict market movements. Decentralised finance (DeFi) platforms are breaking traditional barriers, offering novel ways for transactions and investments, while blockchain interoperability is paving the way for seamless asset exchanges across different networks. Environmental sustainability is emerging as a crucial focus, pushing the industry towards energy-efficient solutions for crypto mining and transaction processing. Embracing these advancements, whilst being vigilant of regulatory shifts, will be key for traders aiming to remain competitive and thrive in the coming era of crypto trading.

Emerging Trends and Technologies

In the fast-paced world of crypto trading, emerging trends and technologies are rewriting the playbook for how traders operate and strategize. The advent of blockchain technology has been a catalyst in reshaping financial ecosystems, and the possibilities it unleashes continue to expand, creating ripples in both nascent and developed markets. Traders who can stay ahead of these trends stand to gain significantly, while those caught off-guard risk being swept away by the rapidly evolving landscape.

One of the most prominent technological advancements impacting crypto trading is the development of decentralised finance, or DeFi. This burgeoning sector leverages blockchain technology to provide financial services without traditional banks acting as intermediaries. DeFi platforms are democratizing access to services such as lending, borrowing, and trading, potentially challenging the hegemony of established financial institutions. For a crypto trader, understanding DeFi protocols can be a game-changer, offering new avenues for investment and speculation.

Simultaneously, the rise of non-fungible tokens (NFTs) is opening up a new frontier in the crypto world. NFTs represent ownership of unique digital items, and their trade is now a booming market. For traders, NFTs aren't just about art; they're an investment class of their own, characterized by high volatility and the potential for significant returns. The strategic buying and selling of NFTs could augment a trader's portfolio, and for those who can discern valuable trends in this domain, the rewards could be substantial.

Another trend reshaping crypto trading is the increasing sophistication of trading algorithms and the use of artificial intelligence. AI is increasingly being deployed to analyse vast amounts of data, providing insights and signals that were previously inaccessible. These technologies can help traders to predict market movements with greater accuracy, allowing for more informed decision-making. Additionally, AI-powered tools are automating routine trading tasks, freeing up time for traders to focus on strategy rather than execution.

Blockchain technology is not just facilitating new types of financial products; it's also enhancing transparency and security in trading operations. With smart contracts, trades can be executed automatically when certain conditions are met, reducing the need for intermediaries and the risks associated with them. This increase in automation results in reduced costs and faster transactions, enhancing the overall efficiency of the markets. For traders, leveraging smart contracts can lead to more robust trading strategies that are less prone to human error.

Furthermore, the development of central bank digital currencies (CBDCs) by various nations is poised to impact crypto trading significantly. As governments explore their own state-backed digital currencies, the ways in which cryptocurrencies and fiat money interact will undoubtedly evolve. This might provide traders with opportunities for arbitrage and new trading pairs, while also bringing about regulatory challenges that will need careful navigation.

On the technical side, scalability solutions such as Layer 2 protocols are gaining traction, addressing some of the limitations of existing blockchain networks. Enhancements like these aim to increase transaction throughput without compromising network security or decentralisation. Improved scalability could increase the adoption of cryptocurrencies in everyday transactions, pushing the demand even further. Traders who are aware of these developments can anticipate shifts in market dynamics and position themselves accordingly.

As mobile technology advances, the ubiquity of smartphones is playing an increasingly vital role in crypto trading. With more users accessing trading platforms via mobile apps, accessibility has never been easier, enabling traders to monitor and execute trades on-the-go. This ease of access also increases participation from a broader audience, which could drive liquidity and contribute to market stability—a boon for those adept at navigating such environments.

Decentralised autonomous organisations (DAOs) represent another cutting-edge development within the crypto space. DAOs are organisations run by smart contracts, where decision-making is decentralized. They are changing the landscape of corporate governance and collective decision-making, offering traders new investment opportunities as they evolve into a viable business model. Tracking the success and failures of DAOs will allow savvy traders to tap into this yet-underexplored potential.

Lastly, the interplay between technology and institutional investment cannot be overlooked. As institutional players enter the market, they bring both liquidity and sophisticated trading techniques. Their presence is often seen as a validation of the crypto ecosystem, encouraging more cautious investors to enter the fray. The influence of institutional trading on market trends and prices should not be underestimated, and traders should be prepared to adapt their strategies in response to these large-scale market movements.

In summary, the emerging trends and technologies in crypto trading are not just enhancing the current trading environment; they are reshaping it entirely. From DeFi and NFTs to AI and DAOs, these innovations are transforming how traders execute transactions, evaluate investments, and even conceive of market opportunities. By staying informed and agile, traders can harness these advancements to their advantage, thus positioning themselves for success in an ever-evolving market. It is with a keen eye on these trends that aspiring traders can navigate the future of crypto trading and seize the opportunities that come with it.

Preparing for the Future of Crypto Trading

As we navigate through the ever-evolving landscape of crypto trading, it's crucial to look ahead and prepare for what the future holds. The realm of crypto trading doesn't stand still. It demands continuous learning and adaptation. As technological advancements alter the contours of this market, traders must anticipate these shifts, so they aren't left behind. In this section, we're going to explore how you can equip yourself with the tools and mindset necessary to thrive amidst future changes.

First and foremost, staying abreast of technological developments is key. Blockchain technology is continually evolving, with new advancements emerging regularly. Be it changes in consensus mechanisms, the scalability of networks, or innovations in smart contract technology, there's always something new on the horizon. Keeping an eye on these developments can provide early insights into potential trading opportunities and challenges. Remember, those who stay informed are better positioned to capitalise on new trends.

Now, imagine the possibilities with AI and machine learning in crypto trading. These technologies are becoming increasingly sophisticated, playing a pivotal role in data analysis and trading strategy formulation. The ability to digest vast amounts of data and identify patterns more rapidly than a human ever could is revolutionary. Consider dedicating time to understand how these technologies can be incorporated into your trading toolkit. Not only does this enhance efficiency, but it also adds a competitive edge in a fast-paced market.

Another factor to consider is regulatory evolution. Crypto regulations are in flux worldwide as governments and institutions attempt to keep pace with the rapid growth of digital assets. While this can add an element of unpredictability, it also provides a framework that, once established, can legitimise and stabilise the market. Approaching regulations with an adaptable mindset will help you mitigate risks and adjust strategies accordingly, ensuring your trading practices align with legal frameworks.

Crossing borders, geographically and metaphorically, the trend of tokenised assets is gaining traction. Tokenisation opens doors to fractional ownership and liquidity in assets like real estate, art, and more. This concept may redefine markets by making them more accessible and diverse. For forward-thinking traders, recognising the implications of tokenised assets can provide a frontier for new strategies and income streams. The time to start researching and understanding this trend is now.

Interoperability between different blockchain networks is another emerging trend with significant implications for future trading. As various blockchain projects seek to bridge their technologies, the exchange of assets and information across networks becomes more fluid. This development can lead to an expansive ecosystem with more efficient trading practices and diversified opportunities. Keeping a pulse on interoperability projects might enhance your capabilities to operate seamlessly across platforms.

Virtual reality and augmented reality may seem like technologies confined to gaming and entertainment, yet they hold potential in the crypto trading realm. Picture immersive trading environments where data is not only visualised but experienced in multidimensional ways. Such advancements could transform how traders interact with and interpret market data. While still in nascent stages, experimenting with these technologies could position you ahead of the curve.

It's vital not to overlook the meteoric rise and influence of digital currencies derived from central bank initiatives, known as Central Bank Digital Currencies (CBDCs). These can reshape national and global financial landscapes significantly, influencing market dynamics in unforeseen ways. Remaining informed about CBDC developments can offer critical insights, enabling traders to adjust their strategies effectively. Patience and careful observation will play a central role here.

Community-driven insights can't be underestimated in the future of crypto trading. Decentralised Autonomous Organisations (DAOs) and community initiatives are not just influencing project governance but also market behaviour. By participating in these communities, traders not only stay informed but also contribute to shaping the future landscape. Engage with DAOs, attend forums, and harness the hive mind's power, which might just give you that needed edge.

Lastly, nurturing a forward-focused trading mindset is uncompromisable. Cultivating resilience, adaptability, and an openness to continuous learning can prepare you for the uncertainties that lie ahead. It's not simply about having the right tools—it's also about being mentally equipped to handle the unpredictable nature of the crypto realm. Leadership, after all, begins with you, and it's this mindset that can transform challenges into gateways for innovation.

In summary, success in the future of crypto trading hinges on staying informed, embracing technological advancements, understanding regulatory landscapes, engaging with new forms of assets and trading environments, and developing an adaptive mindset. By anticipating and preparing for these changes, you can confidently step into the future, ready to seize opportunities and navigate challenges with acumen and vision. The crypto market is vibrant and ever-changing—embrace its dynamic nature, prepare for what's to come, and the future will no longer be a distant horizon but a field ripe with potential.

Conclusion

The journey through this book has equipped you with an expansive toolkit tailored to the ever-evolving world of crypto trading. Just as the crypto market is dynamic and often unpredictable, so too must your approach to it be flexible and informed. Each chapter has offered insights and strategies that, when applied thoughtfully, can lead not just to financial success but to a deeper understanding of market behaviours.

To succeed in crypto trading, it's imperative to develop a keen sense of adaptation. Embracing both fundamental and technical analysis allows you to read not only the numbers presented but the stories those numbers tell. The crypto market, with its unique volatility and extraordinary potential, paints vivid stories through price charts, candlestick patterns, and indicator signals. Recognising these narratives empowers you to anticipate and react to market shifts with precision and confidence.

There's no denying that trading involves risk, but an informed trader is a prudent trader. In the chapters dedicated to risk management and trading psychology, you learned that emotions can be both allies and adversaries. The key is not to eliminate emotion entirely but to manage it effectively. When you strategise with discipline and are prepared for the market's whims, you align yourself closer to consistent profitability.

One cannot underestimate the importance of a solid trading plan. Much like an architect relies on a blueprint, a trader thrives with a well-outlined strategy. A coherent plan provides the structure necessary to navigate trades' uncertainties, guiding you through both prosperous and tumultuous times. Whether you are day trading or holding for the long term, clarity and flexibility are your anchors.

The role of technology in trading also cannot be overstated. From automated trading bots to nuanced indicator combinations, leveraging technology can give you an edge. Yet, technology should complement, not replace, human intuition and judgment. Keeping abreast of emerging trends and technological advancements ensures you stay at the forefront of the crypto landscape, ready to leverage new opportunities as they arise.

Throughout this exploration, the emphasis has been on developing a mindset that thrives on learning. Mastery of crypto trading doesn’t happen overnight; it's a gradual process of understanding, trying, failing, and succeeding. Backtesting and learning from past successes and mistakes are invaluable in honing your skills. In the long run, a committed approach to continuous improvement pays dividends.

Furthermore, remaining vigilant about market news and influences can significantly impact your trading decisions. Becoming adept at distinguishing between market noise and actionable information positions you to make informed decisions amidst the cacophony of media influence. As with many aspects of life, discernment is crucial in crypto trading.

As the landscape of crypto evolves, so must your strategies and perspectives. This adaptability will serve you well, not just in today's market but in preparing for future trends and disruptions. The future of crypto trading is bright, teeming with endless possibilities for those ready to seize them.

Ultimately, the dedication and perseverance you bring to your trading journey are what set you apart. The tools and strategies outlined in this book are merely a starting point, laying a foundation upon which you will build your crypto trading success.

Engage with the material authentically, apply it smartly, and the rewards will follow.

As you forge ahead, always remember that trading is not just a skill but an art. It requires creativity, discipline, and a willingness to innovate. With the knowledge gained from this book and your continued learning, you're poised to not just participate in the crypto market but to excel within it. Here's to your future success in the dynamic world of crypto trading!

Glossary of Crypto Trading Terms

To thrive in the world of crypto trading, it's crucial to familiarise yourself with the language of the market. Below, you'll find an essential glossary of terms that will aid you in navigating the crypto trading landscape with confidence and clarity.

Altcoin

Refers to any cryptocurrency other than Bitcoin. Altcoins include Ethereum, Ripple, Litecoin, and thousands more, each with their own unique features and purposes.

Arbitrage

The practice of taking advantage of price differences between markets to make a profit. In the crypto world, this involves buying on one exchange and selling on another where the price is higher.

Bear Market

A market trend characterised by declining prices. Traders often expect further declines, which can lead to pessimistic market behaviour.

Bull Market

A market trend marked by rising prices. Optimism prevails, as traders expect continued upward movements.

Blockchain

The underlying technology behind cryptocurrencies, blockchain is a decentralised ledger that records all transactions across a network of computers.

FOMO

An acronym for "Fear of Missing Out". In trading, it refers to the anxiety that traders may feel when they fear they aren't capitalising on a profitable move in the market.

FUD

Short for "Fear, Uncertainty, and Doubt". This term describes negative information spread about a cryptocurrency or the market, often intended to dissuade participants or manipulate the market.

HODL

A misspelling of "hold," it refers to the strategy of maintaining a long-term position in a cryptocurrency irrespective of price volatility. It's often used as a rallying cry among enthusiasts.

ICO (Initial Coin Offering)

A method used by startups in the cryptocurrency space to raise funds by offering initial tokens in exchange for investment from early backers.

Liquidity

The ease with which a cryptocurrency can be bought or sold in the market without affecting the price. High liquidity indicates a more stable market.

Market Capitalisation

The total value of a cryptocurrency, calculated by multiplying the current price by the total supply in circulation. It's often used to gauge the relative size of a cryptocurrency.

Pump and Dump

A scheme that involves artificially inflating the price of a cryptocurrency through misleading or exaggerated statements, followed by a rapid sell-off once the price is sufficiently high.

Smart Contract

Self-executing contracts with the terms of the agreement directly written into code. They run on blockchain networks like Ethereum, facilitating trustless and automated transactions.

Stablecoin

A type of cryptocurrency designed to maintain a stable value by being pegged to a reserve asset such as a fiat currency (e.g., USD) or a basket of assets.

Token

A digital asset created on a blockchain platform. Tokens can represent various utilities, be used for transactions, or signify ownership of an asset.

Whale

A term used to describe individuals or entities that hold a large amount of a particular cryptocurrency, often possessing enough to influence market prices with their trading decisions.

By mastering these terms, you'll be better equipped to engage with crypto trading communities and enhance your trading acumen. Remember, the journey in crypto trading is ever-evolving, so keep this glossary handy as you continue to explore and expand your crypto trading expertise.

Made in the USA
Monee, IL
04 November 2026

67386092R10098